Len Airey
On Antarctica

Illustrated by John Elliot

A Luna Books Publication

On Antarctica
Copyright © 2001 by Len Airey

The right of Len Airey to be identified as the author of this work
has been asserted by him in accordance with
Copyright, Designs and Patents Act, 1988

ISBN 0-9708699-0-8

Published in the USA by Luna Books

Printed and bound in the USA by
Falcon Books, San Ramon, California

Photographs by Len Airey
Illustrations by John Elliot
Cover Art by John Elliot
Front: Author, Shackleton and the Endurance
Back: Shelf ice, Halley

1st Edition

www.OnAntarctica.com

Who is the third who walks always beside you?
When I count, there are only you and I together
But when I look ahead up the white road
There is always another one walking beside you
Gliding wrapped in a brown mantle, hooded
I do not know whether a man or a woman
— But who is that on the other side of you?

—T. S. Eliot, *The Waste Land*

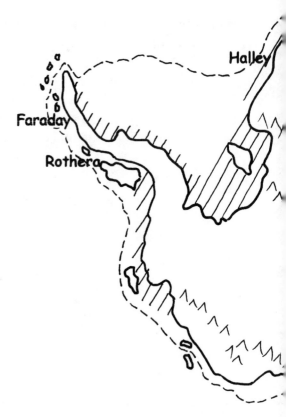

South Georgia

Falkland
Islands

South
America

Faraday

Rothera

Halley

South Pole

On Antarctica

Len Airey was born in Cornwall, England. He graduated at Bath University in Mathematics, and went on to study at Bradford and Heriot-Watt Universities. He lived and worked in Antarctica for four years and was awarded the Polar Medal in 1986 for outstanding services in Antarctica. Since leaving his native home for Antarctica, Len Airey has also lived in Papua New Guinea, Argentina and Venezuela. During his varied career he has worked in the electronics industry, in the Royal Air Force, as a Teacher of Mathematics, with British Antarctic Survey, and as a Safety, Health and Environment Consultant with major oil companies world-wide. He currently lives in Venezuela.

For Ambrose, John and Kevin
For the record

Acknowledgments

Writing is re-writing. And when the manuscript is written, the work begins. A book is a project, and the better you manage the project the better the book. I want to acknowledge those who encouraged me and helped with *On Antarctica*.

I sent *On Antarctica* to countless publishers but with stereotypical replies. However, I feel no resentment against them for saying "no." In fact, it is a better book because of them!

I commissioned the services of The Literary Consultancy (TLC) for a professional review of the text. They also told me what I didn't want to hear. But there was one short paragraph in the report written by them that made the investment in their review worthwhile. They suggested how I could restructure my work into a readable book.

I am indebted to Bill Colquhoun of Technical Editing and Writing Services (TEWS). As well as edit my manuscript, he taught me basic grammar. "Generally, your writing is good. However, if you learned just a few more rules of punctuation and grammar, you would eliminate ninety percent of the work for an editor. Here are the rules I think would be a snap for you ..."

I am extremely grateful to John Elliot for providing all the illustrations and front cover design for *On Antarctica*. John is an accomplished illustrator, artist and film-maker. He has written and illustrated articles for American Artist Magazine, Quarto Books, and is a contributing editor on The Artist's Magazine. He illustrated the popular Reader's Digest Sketching School and is staff illustrator for Classic New Jersey Magazine. Among his commissions are works for Ronald Reagan, Jacqueline Kennedy Onassis and Katherine Hepburn. John and his wife, Sheila, who helped more than she knows, characterised that which I failed to put into words.

I chose Falcon Books to print my work. They helped me through the maze of technical jargon and select the correct materials for *On Antarctica*. Their attention to detail produced a high-quality book that is a must for any adventure travel collection.

All the photographs that appear in *On Antarctica* were taken and processed by myself on Ektachrome slide film. They were developed in Antarctica using Ektachrome process kits. Despite watermarks, hairs and dust on the slides after years of storage, Mac McDougald of Doogle Digital transformed them into their current form.

I am grateful to Ranulph Fiennes for his generousity in providing the foreword.

Finally, I would like to say thank you to my family and friends who read the script. They were honest in their appraisal of the book, and they encouraged me to continue and publish *On Antarctica*.

Len Airey

Foreword

On Antarctica is a very private book, yet a very open revelation of a man who lived his dream for a while. Len Airey yearns to following in the wake of early Antarctic explorers. "I had been determined to stand where Ernest Shackleton had once stood in Antarctica," he writes. And when he stood on South Georgia, the final resting place for Shackleton, he makes the commentary, "I recalled what Shackleton had said when he received the news that Scott had died attempting to be the first man to reach the South Pole. "He did not mean to die in Europe. He wanted (some day) to die away on one of his expeditions and I shall go on going, old man, 'till one day I shall not come back."

But On Antarctica is not concerning history. The author endures the very best and the very worst imaginable during four long years. It is a frank, sometimes agonizing account of his interaction with the continent and comrades. "The landscape slowly took on its winter coat as sea and land became one. . . ", and "He loomed up at me like a Rottweiler. The others backed away. He put his face close to mine. . . " Each of his three winters living on remote research stations is very different. Fear, excitement, debauchery, camaraderie, the joy of isolation, and above all the wonder of the place are all well covered in this fascinating story, which is well served by the excellent illustrations of artist John Elliot.

Sir Ranulph Twisleton-Wykeham-Fiennes Bt OBE

On Antarctica

"Mr Airey," began EMPS. He was strabismus—one eye focused on me and the other, high towards the ceiling. "Are you interested in furthering your career as an Ionosphericist, or are you just trying to get yourself a passage to Antarctica?" he asked. I sank into my seat and looked back at the four interviewers before me. The bridge to my dream was collapsing. EMPS knew, I knew, almost the whole world knew that I had no career as an Ionosphericist. I could hardly spell the damn word. In fact, I had looked it up in the dictionary only the day before and paraphrased its definition.

"Mr Salmon, Sir ..." But I could hardly bring myself to say it. The dream would not come true. If only they knew how much I wanted this ...

"Mr Salmon, I have to be honest with you." My foot was almost on the interview table. I pulled at my sock, annoyed with my failure. I thought of that long, lonely train journey home. But there was nothing else to say. It was over. "I would do anything, Sir — cook, paint ... anything. I just wanted to go to Antarctica!" I purposely used the past tense. I knew the next step, towards the door. I was a grown man, almost in tears. EMPS smiled. He was a charismatic person who knew what he was looking for. They all smiled, and they were looking at me. They sat back in their chairs and smiled at each other, and at that moment I knew. I knew that I was going to Antarctica.

Thank you EMPS — Eric M.P. Salmon, Personnel Officer, British Antarctic Survey 1980.

FID
AT
FARADAY

The Bransfield's one hundred-metre crimson hull, strengthened for ice conditions, her hold and decks laden with cargo, turned into the Lemaire Channel. On either side of the vessel in the narrow strait loomed titanic cliffs of ice. Seals, curious to inspect the new arrival, popped their heads up through the icy blue, calm water. We had arrived in Antarctica. The decks were a hive of activity as the crew prepared for work.

It had been a long voyage. Two eventful months had passed since I looked back from the ship as tugboats pulled us out into deeper water from Southampton dock. There were crying sisters, girl friends promising to wait, distraught mums, proud dads "That's my lad," and envious young brothers. My emotions were replaced by joy and excitement as the dockside figures disappeared from view and the voyage had finally begun. What were two and a half years between loved ones? Two and a half years before I saw home again. Home—I had no home. All that I possessed was packed into three cardboard boxes left behind in some attic, things that had no use in Antarctica. I had shed the old skin, the routine. I was starting anew. I quit the career job and put everything behind me. I felt as free as the seabirds that followed our wake.

We neared an island, in fact, a small group of islands — huge glaciers, deceptively close, swept down from the Antarctic mainland. The first indication of human presence in this wilderness of ice, rock and sea was a tattered Union Jack lying limp on its pole. At first it was hard to see the huts hidden behind a mass of ice and snow, but slowly they came into view. There was a bright-red British telephone box on a rock out to sea. It looked bizarre. It was obviously a joke, and it had been erected in our honour. I had arrived at Faraday, my new home. But, for the first time since leaving the old life, I felt some misgivings. I stared at the dull collection of old, blackened, wooden huts that were surrounded by a fairy tale land of ice. The base appeared insignificant, cold and unfriendly in the beautiful massive landscape. Diesel had leaked from an old storage tank and stained the rocks below. The constant drone from the base's electrical generator spoilt the silent surroundings. Littered among the buildings were dumps of materials, skidoos and essential equipment too large to store inside. They were loosely covered with bright orange tarpaulins, some almost hidden by what remained of the winter snow. Piles of empty beer barrels and an ugly array of communication aerials contributed to the disorderly appearance of the base. Skis were stuck randomly into a pile of snow near the entrance. Thirty years of occupation had left its mark on Antarctica. This was not the Hilton; not even the Hilton's gardening shed.

Captain Lawrence gave a long blast on the ship's horn as he manoeuvred his vessel into place, close to the Faraday shoreline. Chain rattled as the anchor dropped through the heavy brash ice surrounding the ship in shallow water. The ship was close to rocks and awesome looking icebergs—not a position many captains would consider anchoring a 5,000-ton vessel, with or without ice breaking capability.

I stared across to the uninviting hut from my vantage point on deck. A pipe that led from the base down to the shoreline spilled water into the sea. It was obvious where the sewage went by the number of birds that carefully examined the outlet. It was easy to imagine the sight when the sea froze over in the winter! The shoreline was deserted apart from the birds. I expected to have seen a welcoming party—people waving and jumping with joy at the return of the ship. After all, it was nearly a year since the Bransfield last visited Faraday, and for some the two and a half years of life on base were over! The scow was made ready for landing as I stared in misbelief; there was nobody in sight. I grew more apprehensive. I was not prepared for this. They must have known we were here!

"We're here! It's over!" I wanted to shout, "We've brought your mail! Look—fresh vegetables, mail, beer...you can go home!"

The shore remained silent. For an instant I thought that some catastrophe had befallen them. I wondered what effect the isolation of two long winters must have had. What effect would it have on me? What would they look like and how would they behave? Would I run down to meet the ship this time next year?

The scow and a launch were lowered into the icy water, and events started to escalate. There had been two months of reading, drinking, eating and sleeping, inactivity on a mammoth scale while travelling south. The ship's crane swung into action. First a net of keg beer, then post bags, fresh fruit, vegetables and "high priority" cargo were all lowered into the scow. Someone gave the signal, and I climbed down a rope ladder slung over the side of the ship and found somewhere to sit among the cargo. I felt odd in my new FID clothes, a beginner, an upstart and inexperienced. I didn't look the part, like an Antarctic explorer should. The launch strained pulling the laden scow as we made our way through the thick brash ice towards the shore.

No sooner had we landed than a mass of tangled blonde hair, frayed clothing and huge blackened rubber boots swaged his way from the base and down the slipway towards us. The figure looked more ape-like than human. He merely grunted some sort of welcome and looked at us indifferently as we struggled to get out of the scow onto the slippery concrete. A pair of spectacles peered at us through the tangle of hair. Don was a Faraday FID and had been one for just one year. There was no telling if his time on base had changed him, but he did not look or react normally. I learnt that Don was not due to leave the base; he had another winter to face. We had a winter to face together. Would I be a shaggy ape this time next year?

Other FIDS soon emerged from the base all dressed similar to Don, wearing Antarctic-style clothing issued by British Antarctic Survey (BAS). FIDS (Falkland Island Dependencies Survey) was the early name used by BAS. Now, however, FIDS meant *Fucking Idiots Down South*. And I was beginning to see why. The FIDS made a long line from the scow to the door of the base. They didn't communicate with us; they hardly acknowledged our presence. They were old hands and knew the routine, getting ready to move the cargo from the scow. We were summoned to join the human chain as scow after scow of cargo came ashore in carefully packed, clearly labelled, almost manageable-sized boxes.

"Give me two," shouted Bob Swan, a burly FIDlet who had travelled south with us and was destined for Rothera, a BAS base further south. He was obsessed with bodybuilding. Someone piled a box onto each of his broad shoulders. He staggered up the slipway, ignoring the chain, much to the amusement of the rest of us. Already built like an upside down triangle, he was intent on getting his frame even bigger. We mere mortal souls stayed in line and carried what we could. It took three days of exhaustive work before all the Faraday cargo was piled high at various sites in and around the base and had been covered with bright orange tarpaulins.

The Bransfield left to complete her itinerary and would return in a few weeks, at the end of the Antarctic summer, to make her final call before the onset of winter. There were thirty of us cramped into the tiny hut designed to accommodate sixteen people at most. The base was alive with activity. Summer headquarter staff were assessing the successes and failures of the previous winter programme. Seasoned FIDS were teaching the new FIDlets and bonding relationships before the onset of winter. FIDS who had "done their time" and whose minds were on other things, they had what seemed a lifetime of plans to get on with. The stresses, trials and tribulations of the previous winter were obvious. The FIDS were adjusting to our arrival and new company.

There were insufficient bunks for everyone, so I chose to sleep in a pyramid tent pitched on ice close to the base. This would be my home for the next couple of months until the Bransfield returned to take away the non-winterers. That would make room for me on base. The weather was far from cold, hovering slightly above freezing point most of the time. The sun barely dipped below the horizon at night, and Antarctica was never dark during those summer months. I was in more danger of overheating than freezing in my cosy bed of sheepskin mattress, airbed and down-filled sleeping bag. I lay in bed at night with the tent door open, looking across to the spectacular mountains on the Antarctic mainland. I had arrived and felt at home.

There was no shortage of work to be done during the following few weeks of summer. The piles of relief cargo had to be sorted, distributed and stored on base. New records and books were enthusiastically received in the bar. A year's supply of frozen, dried and tinned food was shelved below the kitchen in what looked like a well-stocked supermarket. New equipment and spares were stuffed into laboratories and workshops. The floor of the hut groaned under the weight of huge piles of beer, wines and spirits. Everything had its place, spare razors, washing powder, sewing needles, additional clothing … everything was supplied that we were expected to need for the following winter on base. Boxes and packing materials were everywhere, and it took the whole summer before the base began to look liveable again. Emergency supplies were stored in an old hut well away from the main cluster. This food, clothing and equipment would be used in the event of a base catastrophe – the most likely scenario being a major fire.

Builders, plumbers and electricians had worked at Faraday the previous winter to carry out a complete refurbishment of the base. But a lot of work still remained. The more we achieved during the summer with the many people on base, the less we needed to complete when we were left alone to face the winter. Everyone was required to contribute and complete as much of the work as possible, particularly outside work, before the onset of winter storms. The doctor or meteorologist might be a carpenter's mate one day and a plumber, electrician or mechanic's mate the next. FIDS became jack-of-all-trades. New double-glazed windows were installed, and the old wooden structure of the base was clad in bright green, plastic-coated metal sheets to protect the ageing wood underneath. Aerials were repaired. And the rocks and ice surrounding the base were cleaned of rubbish before the winter snow re-covered them. These were not jobs for individuals, but work for the whole base. We were all expected to contribute as well as to complete our individual tasks. We worked together and got along just fine — at least for now! We were assessing each other; but, for the moment, it was easy to avoid the irritants with so many people on base.

There was scientific work to be done. Faraday had a purpose, the study of atmospheric sciences. I was employed as an Ionosphericist, or Beastie-man as we were known. I used the

Beastie, which looked as though it should (and later did) belong
in the British Science Museum, to monitor ionospheric conditions two hundred kilometres above the Antarctic Peninsula. It
was an antiquated piece of equipment, a vertical incidence radar. But the Beastie's assortment of bicycle chains, huge thermi-
onic valves, resistors, capacitors and circuitry dating from the
Edwardian period carried out its function well — although its
transmissions interfered with anything and everything electronic on base. But my mind was rarely on science. I often gazed
through the window of the Beastie room across to Mount Peary,
a three thousand-metre peak that dominated our view of the
Antarctic mainland seven or eight kilometres from our island
home. The base was shadowed to the east by the spectacular
range of mountains that form the ice-covered Antarctic Peninsula, and I was determined to be among them.

I spent days working on the ageing Beastie in an attempt to
improve its performance. I had brought with me a recondi-
tioned receiver I acquired while training at Leicester University
in preparation for my journey south. It still stank of the rat urine
embedded into its ancient components, but it worked well.

Like everyone else on Faraday, I occasionally needed a break
from base routine. An ideal place to spend a night off base was at
Wordie, an abandoned base on one of the many tiny islands adjacent to Faraday. I took great solace in spending nights in the
old hut with a radiant coal fire, a bottle of *hooch*, my favorite music and my guitar. Letters written during my many solitary visits
to the derelict building must have been full of sentimental
thoughts. Sitting at night in front of the old coal stove with a paraffin Tilley lamp hissing away in the background, I could easily
imagine how life had been for the early FIDS in that cramped
dark hut full of smoke from the stove where cooking, eating and
sleeping were all done in the one room. How different life must
have been in those early days of Antarctic exploration.

Telephone communications were non-existent at Faraday. Modern satellite technology had not arrived at BAS bases. There was reluctance by BAS to allow the use of telephones in the belief that communication would make the long contracts imposed on the FIDS harder to endure. Messages were punched out on paper tape and fed over the radio to Cable and Wireless on the Falkland Islands — a telex link. Cable and Wireless in Stanley passed the messages on to their station on Ascension Island. It passed them on to some UK-based Cable and Wireless coastal station, which, in turn, passed them on to BAS at Cambridge Headquarters. From there the private messages were passed on to our families who, if lucky, received the same message we wrote days before. Each of us was restricted by BAS to sending or receiving just one hundred words per month over the telex link. But even with just a hundred words, it was sometimes a struggle to know what to say. "I love you and will see you in two and a half years. We saw penguins and seals today. Say hello to Spot the dog and her new pups for me. Get me ouuuuuuuut of here!"

I wanted the summer to end and the Bransfield to come and take away the people who were due to leave. I wanted to be left alone and to get on with the winter, as did the other few that would remain. But we were busy during those early summer weeks, and time passed quickly. I went outdoors travelling around the island group as often as my commitment to work and the weather would allow. Skiing was popular and great exercise. But the snow was soft, and the sea ice from the previous winter had melted. So I had to think of something else to occupy my leisure time. I built myself a sub-aqua wet-suit and took to the sea. The water was less than one degree Celsius but bearable in the rubber suit. I wallowed in the water for hours, playing on and under great chunks of ice floating close to the base. The air was fresh, the sun shone and the scenery was awe-inspiring. Where else could I have all this at my doorstep. I found two old canoes stored beneath one of the huts and often paddled around the many creeks that separated the group of islands, exploring every bit of my new environment.

"Heeeeeeeelp!" screamed Ambrose as we paddled together one Sunday morning. He was a pimply faced youth with piercing blue eyes and regarded combing his hair or shaving as a great inconvenience. He was just twenty years old, straight out of college and unable to grow anything more than a trace of a beard. We travelled south together from Rio de Janeiro. Ambrose was a late recruit and missed the first leg of the voyage from Southampton. Despite his nervous disposition, boyish face and complete lack of work experience, he managed his responsibilities well as the base radio operator. Ironically, we had both studied to be radio operators at Southampton, but my studies ended when Ambrose was just five years old! Despite our difference in age, we got on well.

"Heeeeeeeelp!" he screamed. His canoe rocked heavily and then rose in the air. We were in heavy brash ice in Meek Channel, a narrow opening between islands. Brash ice is fragmented ice that covers the surface of the sea like crushed ice in a cocktail. I headed my canoe towards Ambrose's when a great, black, spotted head rose from the sea between us. Huge, dark, glossy eyes first looked at me. Then its great head spun through one hundred and eighty degrees and focused on Ambrose before diving again. It was a "playful" Leopard seal, the terror of every penguin and baby seal in Antarctica. It again swam under Ambrose's canoe and bounced him up and down in the water. I was terrified it would turn on me.

"Heeeeeeeelp, heeeeeeeelp!"

"For fuck sake shut up, Ambrose." I banged furiously at the water with my paddle in an attempt to frighten the beast away. I looked down through the crystal clear water and saw the spotted, shinning black carnivore laying on its back at the bottom of the creek looking up at us. I could have sworn that it was grinning, enjoying the moment and playing a game with us. I sat motionless, praying that the monster would either go away or be satisfied with playing games with Ambrose. The only recorded attack by a Leopard seal on a man was when an early Antarctic explorer hit one on the head with a hammer to kill it for dog meat. This practice might work well on other seals, but it had no effect on the thick scull of the Leopard. Presumably the ill informed explorer mistook it for another species. He was lucky to survive to tell the tale. Ambrose came close to becoming the second person to go down on record as being attacked by a Leopard seal. After what seemed an interminable wait we decided that the seal was either bored or had gone off to look for a more appetising prey. Canoeing declined in popularity as a base activity after the incident.

It was New Year's eve. The festive season in Antarctica is June 21st, mid-winter, significant because summer is closer, the days get longer and the ship's return ever nearer. Even so, New Year's eve was a good excuse for a banquet, party hats, pulling a few crackers and more alcohol. I sat in the bar with the ingredients to make Rum and Cokes while waiting for dinner to be served. Drinking was more than a base social occasion; it was a necessity, a habit. On reflection, we drank extraordinary quantities of alcohol. Don joined me and poured himself a drink. He was one of the easiest of base members to get along with. He wore a one-piece, bright red, combination long-john and vest with a Captain Bligh party hat. This was Don's formal dinner attire, with the exception of the Captain Bligh hat. He never wore it at any other time, except on very special occasions. It was time for pre-dinner aperitifs, time to warm up before the banquet began. It was a day of heavy responsibility for the cook.

"What was the name of the ship in *Mutiny on the Bounty*?" asked Don, helping himself to another Rum and Coke.

I paused and looked at him suspiciously. When sober, Don was not an eccentric; he was an ape-like met-man, a meteorologist. But after four Rum and Cokes he became a philosopher, a thinker of complicated thoughts simply phrased. For his young age, Don knew a lot. I had great respect for his knowledge.

"Tough one, Don," I replied as he poured himself another Rum and Coke. "The name of the ship in *Mutiny on the Bounty*. Hm! ... Bounty?" I replied, cautiously.

I watched him drink yet another Rum and Coke. Of course, Don could drink at least ten without being in the least bit drunk, but four was a mystic number with him, a dividing line. He slapped his fourth glass down on the bar.

"Bollocks!" he said. Eye spectacles made a rare appearance through his hair, and he flashed his eyes at me. Then he repeated, "Bollocks."

Don was becoming philosophical. I decided to experiment to see if he really had drunk four glasses. "Why is Bounty not the right answer, Don?" I asked, genuinely concerned.

"Bollocks," he said.

"Mutiny?" I guessed, expecting some strange twist to the question.

"Bollocks...bollocks and more...bollocks!" he said with a long pause between each word before leaving me alone at the bar. Don had reached a higher level and became philosophical early in the evening. I learned more new facts from him that night before we raised our glasses to toast the New Year. The base was partying and celebrated January 1st, 1981.

The Antarctic party had only just begun ...

With January came the tourists, yachtsmen and military. The HMS Endurance, the only British military vessel to operate in Antarctica, brought the first of what seemed an endless stream of visitors. She anchored overnight. We were visited by such distinguished guests as Rex Hunt, the Governor of the Falkland Islands, Pebble Mill at One, a television team researching a documentary, and Lord and Lady Buxton, the heads of Anglia TV. Their mission was to save the Endurance. The British Government had decided to scrap the vessel, considering it unnecessary to patrol the southern seas and necessary to make savings in the military budget. Rex Hunt thought otherwise. Outspoken against the British decision, he was on a mission to find support for his cause — to protect the Falkland Islands against threat from Argentina. Removing the Endurance would hinder his concern. But we saw his visit as another excuse to party. Not without event, his mission at Faraday ended early the next morning when the Endurance left, heading north.

But no sooner had the Endurance exited through Lemaire Channel than the first tourist vessel arrived.

"Its the World Discover," reported Ambrose. "They want to send umpteen tourists ashore!"

The vessel was a luxury ship for the rich and those on a last fling with whatever money was left over in their retirement funds. At first I resented them. Here I was trying to be *roughie toughie* and a bunch of geriatric tourists was coming ashore with all the luxuries we were trying to escape. We received the news with mixed blessing. Some thought that we should discourage them, others hid in the work sites, while others sat in the bar and commenced another drinking session – or, rather, continued the one from the Endurance's visit. However, it was clear that base life was going to be disrupted by the visit, and most work came to a halt. In fact, once started, the spontaneous party went well into the following day.

Twenty at a time, wearing bright red windproof coats and lifejackets, the tourists invaded the base. Despite there being more than a hundred of them, they managed to cram into the Faraday bar and get plenty of alcohol and homemade goodies down their throats while we impressed them with our roughie toughie FID talk.

"Last veek you 'av much fuck?" asked a little old German lady.

"No," I replied, a little surprised by her question.

"Last veek we 'av very much fuck!" she informed me. Her expressionless face did not show whether or not she understood the significance of her remark.

I imagined the orgy on the ship, rich and naked bodies in the sauna as the vessel penetrated Antarctica. "Fuck," I thought. "This is a base full of men, not bent gents. But no, she means fog, the lady is asking if we had any fog!"

"Ah, yes," I replied politely. "There was a lot of fog here too last week."

She returned my smile. The party raged in the bar, and the tourists photographed everyone and everything in site. But as abruptly as it had all begun, so it ended. The tour operators stopped the party and called everyone back to the ship. They had a schedule to meet, and we were just part of that schedule. We were invited to visit the ship. Their Geminis were loaded with tourists and drunken FIDS, and we made our way through the brash ice back to the World Discoverer.

I was drunk, very drunk, and found myself in the middle of a luxury bar being served cocktails by waiters fit for the Hilton. I looked back towards the base. What the hell am I doing here? I was dressed in my FID gear. A couple danced on the dance floor while the band played *Waltzing Matilda*. I thought of the Titanic, how people had sat in a similar bar as an iceberg ripped into her hull. My head was swirling, and I wanted to vomit. I was beckoned over to a nearby table where two well-dressed ladies sat, smiling at me.

"I'm Judith," said a large, buxom girl introducing herself. "And this is my friend Sally," she said, patting her friend on the head.

"Please, join us," beckoned Sally.

I sat next to Judith, and a waiter arrived to take my order. "Rum and Coke, please."

The band played on. But the FIDS weren't dancing; they were drinking. The ladies were very warm towards me. I looked down at Judith's huge breasts. It was not so many months since I last had sex, but there were many, many more months ahead before I would again know the pleasure of a woman.

"Who's that?" Judith asked, pointing to Don in his one-piece, bright red, combination long-john and vest, but minus his Captain Bligh party hat.

Don was pulling faces at the flute player, trying to make him laugh and blow a wrong note as the ballroom filled with the orchestra's rendition of Mozart's Magic Flute.

"That's Don. He's a philosopher," I replied, estimating that Don had well passed the mystic number of Rum and Cokes and was no longer a met-man.

Judith, Sally and I danced, drank, talked and laughed our way through the evening. We could have been on a ship anchored anywhere in the world for all I cared. Antarctica was forgotten. The spectacular views through the ship's windows embroidered with velvet curtains mattered not one iota to me at the time, and the rest of the FIDS were also long past caring. Don had given up on the flute player and, instead, was arguing with Ambrose. They were putting the world to right. Ambrose loved a good bar session.

Egged on by the aroma of perfume, by drink and dancing closer than normal, I felt horny. It had been a long time. I pressed closer to Judith. Don had passed out horizontal in front of the band, and the waiters politely stepped over him.

"You take him," said Sally. "You're much closer to a divorce than I am."

Judith nodded and smiled at me. A feeling that I had not experienced for a long time shot through my body. I wondered where her husband was as we hurried down the corridor to her cabin. The adequate double bed beckoned, and we started to kiss passionately. I squeezed one of her huge breasts. The effect was electric. But no sooner had it all begun …

"All FIDS ashore in two minutes," bellowed some well-meaning steward who I will hate for the rest of my life, ruining Judith's chance of tourism with a difference in Antarctica and probably my last chance for years.

No sooner had the World Discoverer upped anchor and disappeared into French Passage when a yacht motored into Stella Creek. It dropped anchor, and four hairy looking Frenchmen came ashore in a rubber dinghy. Claude, Michelle, Bruno and Daniel had left France five years ago in this fifteen metres of steel hull called Kim. They were stopping off at Faraday before returning to France.

"Wes are going to vinter at de ald Petermann ut," they announced. "Wes will den go back to France and make good a book and film to make us reech and buy new boat.... Ha, ha, ha!"

They did not smell exactly like Frenchmen, but they did smell! The odour of garlic and Gitanes was definitely there; but it was mixed with the smell of paraffin, fish and other things, which I preferred not to identify.

Permann hut was an abandoned Argentine station just a few kilometres from Faraday. The news that we would have neighbours during the winter was not well received by some of the FIDS who were due to stay over that winter. In fact, there was sheer hostility towards the French by some. Having neighbours just twelve kilometres away on the adjacent Petermann Island was not some FIDS' idea of being isolated in Antarctica. I suspected that they were envious, or even jealous, that the French were on a bigger adventure than they were. However, personally, I found it intriguing that yachtsmen could fare such far-flung seas. We had crossed Drake's Passage in the Bransfield, but in a yacht …

We had sailed nearly six thousand miles before reaching the feared Roaring Forties. I had recalled accounts of epic voyages by early Antarctic explorers, lone sailors and ships that had got into trouble rounding Cape Horn in dramatic seas. But I thought that was all in the past. I never imagined yachts like Kim still lived those adventures. But they had done it, unscathed in forty feet of steel. I remembered how the wind and heavy seas had battered our ship during the voyage. Kim would also have experienced the Grey Headed, Wandering and Black Brow Albatross; the Giant, White Chinned and Storm Petrels; the Dominican gulls, and the Cape Pigeon that had followed patiently in our wake waiting for the kitchen gash to be tossed overboard. What must they have felt as they passed their first iceberg as it dwarfed their tiny yacht? Our first, unforgettable sighting of the majestic, powerful islands of ice was spectacular. Birds soared above the gargantuan, towering, crystal cliffs as their mammoth bulk seemingly ignored the effect of wind and waves. These ghostly white icons slowly drifted towards their final destiny. Even in an overcast sky, the 30-metre walls of glistening blue ice, topped by layers of snow, shone pure white. As we sailed closer to Antarctica the sea temperature dropped dramatically and its colour changed from dark to light blue. We had entered the Antarctic convergence where the glacial melt waters converged with the sea, reducing the salinity of the water and causing the change in colour. We had seen all this from the comparative comfort of a large ship ... but to have done it in a yacht ... I wanted to know more about these adventurers, these men of the sea.

Someone must have beaten the jungle drums and announced a French open day on Faraday. The following morning a second French yacht, Isasis, arrived with a very respectable couple, Jean and Claudine. Claudine was heavily pregnant. Like the Frenchmen on Kim, they lived at sea, gypsies of the seas of the world. They wanted to stay the winter at Leith, an abandoned whaling station close to Grytviken on South Georgia, hundreds of miles north of Faraday.

"It's that way," I said, pointing north. "Just follow the Endurance." Where did these people come from? What were they doing here? My Antarctic world had been turned upside down.

"Claudine vill ave our baby zer and I vill pull it out. Ve French do not need ospitals," Jean informed me. The crew of Kim agreed. The French had a different way of doing things.

I flinched. But it was getting late in the summer, and the sea ice would soon form around Faraday, giving us the responsibility of "pulling it out" and an extra visitor over the winter.

Isasis was a dreamboat with all the modern facilities — aluminium hull, retractable keel, self-rigging and an automatic pilot

strong enough to navigate the yacht through the worst of storms. She was big, strong and very expensive. The crew of Kim was deeply envious when they saw it, and so was I. Kim left to make a winter home at nearby Petermann while Isasis left to have a baby alone.

I became fascinated, overawed and deeply envious of these yachtsmen's tales of adventure and intrigue. I could never have imagined routinely sailing to Antarctica, circumnavigating the globe, stopping where winds take you, for as long as your heart lets you. Had I found my next adventure after Antarctica? Could I do what they were doing? They made it sound easy. I probed them for information: What type of yacht, what equipment, where, how and when? I began to read everything I could about sailing.

I began to think about the end of my two winters in Antarctica, even before the first had begun.

3

We partied for what seemed like weeks, but I was getting restless for the mountains that were so temptingly close. On those long Antarctic days when the sun shone over the glaciers, I scanned the silvery peaks for routes to their summits. Adventure had dominated my life — caving, mountaineering, hang-gliding and skiing. I loved the open air — yachts, horses, canoes, mountain-bikes and all places silent. I was a global gypsy, a recluse in exile. I had inflicted on myself a most crowded solitude imaginable. My Great Spirit told me to fill my rucksack with two weeks of provisions and explore forest and mountain tracks alone, but that was not to be. I was a loner, a

part-time hermit, and a worshiper of nature. But BAS permitted each FID just short periods away from base, normally no longer than seven days at a time, to travel to some adjacent islands or to climb certain mountains on the mainland. There were severe travel restrictions designed to protect us from the unquestionable dangers of living in such an environment. The restrictions were designed to reduce disruption to their scientific programme. But, at the same time, BAS recruited people who wanted to see Antarctica. They recruited young, skilled adventurers. They monitored our travel activities closely, sanctioning travel only to recognised destinations and making sure that no one spent more than a total of fifteen or twenty days away from base each year. Some were critical of the restrictions. For others the restrictions made no difference; they had no intention of leaving the comparative security of the base and becoming exposed to danger.

The mountains beckoned me. I was a mountaineer, skilled in its techniques. But I lacked experience on awesome peaks like my monumental, icy neighbours. I studied old base travel reports. I scoured the glaciers for lines to pass their gaping chasms. I wanted to explore the interior of the mountains and scale the highest peaks where no man had stood. They were frightening but challenging. We were on the fringe of virgin territories. But who would accompany me? Who on base had the experience? There would be no rescue, no search if we went missing. We had only ourselves to get us out of trouble, and most had no mountaineering experience at all.

Before we left for Antarctica, BAS had brought us together for a week of survival training on the Derbyshire granite cliffs. It was only then that I met all the FIDS who would be going south with me. There were doctors, carpenters, mechanics, cooks, plumbers, climbers and other scientists. Amongst them were geologists and biologists, some of whom I had seen in the corridors of BAS headquarters.

Experienced FIDS led the event, helped by new recruit mountaineering experts such as Steve Taite, John Anderson and other General Assistants (GAs). They were experienced climbers bound for Rothera to accompany geologists while they scoured the continent for rock and ice samples. It was a fun event but the techniques taught were all many would have to keep them alive once away from their Antarctic bases.

We were an unusual assortment of individuals. Many had already some admirable achievements to their name, particularly in mountaineering. Roger Meyer and John Anderson had ascended the north face of the Eiger and other big mountain walls. They saw BAS as a way to make mountaineering pay and, at the same time, further their sport in Antarctica. Others, such as Bob Swan and the Faraday doctor, Mike Stroud, had ambition for fame and saw BAS as a possible passport to their goals. They had a hidden agenda that was later to emerge in spectacular style. There was vast mountaineering experience among the FIDS, but little of it at Faraday.

Caches of emergency food and camping equipment were stored at strategic locations within the travel area, and one good excuse to travel was to check the condition of the dumps, replacing supplies if necessary.

Summer travel by sea, as distinct from winter travel over sea ice, normally involved four people in two fibreglass dinghies. A ten-foot open fibreglass dinghy powdered by a small Seagull outboard engine at sea among the icebergs was risky. We carried a second, spare outboard in each dinghy as back up and had radios, camping, climbing and cooking equipment, and sufficient food for at least fourteen days in the field. But it was still risky. Driving the boats between icebergs and under falling glaciers, we were ants among giants.

Mike Stroud, Andy Knox (a met-man) and I decided to go to the base of Mount Peary about fifteen kilometres away on the mainland. It was the highest peak in the area — a mountain of ice and snow that rose up from near sea level to peak at two thousand metres, joining a high-level plateau that ran down the backbone of the Antarctic Peninsula. It looked and was a formidable mountain, continually avalanching into the glaciers below. But its summit was not included in the limits of travel permitted by BAS ever since three Faraday FIDS perished there four of five years earlier. At the time of the accident, a reconnaissance aircraft spotted what was believed to be their bivouac, a bright red sheet spread out on a ledge just below the summit. The final radio communication from them reported that they had reached the summit and were beginning their descent to a base camp at the foot of the mountain, which they had left the same day. From reports at the time, air temperatures dropped dramatically as they began their descent. Nothing more was heard from them, and it was presumed that they were forced to bivouac near the summit and froze to death during the night. Their bodies were never recovered. We intended to camp at the base of Peary, maybe explore a little way up the summit route, and maybe …

Mike and Andy, like myself, were both experienced mountaineers. Mike was our medical doctor and the only person to be given a one-winter contract with BAS. He was not tall, but powerful in every respect. His strong, likeable personality made him one of the more popular base members. He was more intellectual than most. He grinned as he spoke, normally in a loud, commanding voice. He had strong opinions on most things and was very critical of the BAS travel restrictions. He felt cramped by his job, treating minor cuts and bruises, and was carrying out a physiology programme that he didn't believe in. We were his guinea pigs, but he was looking for adventure. He was excited about the prospect of getting off base and into the mountains. Andy was similar in personality to Mike. Son of an Edinburgh University professor, he was bright and quickly frustrated by the confined base environment. He found his job as met-man routine and boring. He was a young, tall, strong Scotsman straight from the university. By his build you could imagine he played on the university rugby team. He was balding in his early years but wore a thickset beard to make up for it. Andy could be loud and critical and, like Mike, struggled with the BAS travel regulations. I had travelled south with both of them on the Bransfield, and we formed a close bond with common interests.

We loaded up our dinghies and set off on the eight-kilometre journey to the mainland, taking us past towering icebergs and through a lot of worrying brash ice. The air was so clear that mountains fifty or sixty kilometres away appeared to be five times closer. Time after time the fragile fibreglass hulls smashed into iron-hard pieces of ice, barely noticeable among the harmless smaller pieces of brash. The dinghies were surprisingly resilient. We were intruders in this desolate place, breaking the isolation with our noisy, smelly little outboard motors. But the seals and penguins barely noticed us pass by, opening one eye at most before returning to sleep on their islands of floating ice.

We hauled the dinghies ashore over a narrow strip of rock that protruded from under a mass of ice at Rasmussen. Here a steep ramp of ice provided less than easy access to the glaciers above. There were few places along the coast where it was possible to reach the mountains above. High seracs of ice, where the glaciers tumbled into the sea at the end of a long journey, formed impassable barriers.

Our rucksacks were heavy. Mike led up the ramp, his crampons barely penetrating the rock-hard ice. Once at the top he secured a fixed rope, making the climb easier for Andy and me. Once we were all above the ramp, we roped together, put on our mountaineering skis and made our way up towards the mountains. We skirted below the summit of Mount Mill, a prominent finger of rock easily identifiable from Faraday. Then we went up the edge of the Bussey Glacier to reach the base of Mount Peary in the late afternoon. The climb had been exhilarating in perfect weather. Even through a thick layer of sun cream the sun bronzed our skin. The stench of the cream became a familiar part of travel. My body warmed to it like the aroma of a hot roast dinner. When I smelled the cream, I knew it was time for play. It had been a long day, and darkness would fall before long. Andy and Mike worked at the frozen tent while I erected an aerial for the radio.

"Faraday, Faraday, this is foxtrot alpha bravo, over," I called base.

"Foxtrot, alpha bravo, read you loud and clear, over," replied Ambrose almost immediately. I could imagine the mess in his radio room, paper everywhere.

"Ambrose, we have reached the base of Peary and will set up camp here for the night on the edge of the Bussey Glacier, over."

"Len, bad news I'm afraid. Runner and Bobby are at Petermann hut with the Kim. They're helping organise the hut to be ready for the winter. But Runner has taken ill, and they need Mike there immediately to attend to him, over."

Neil Shaw had earned the name Runner after escaping from a young lady in Rio de Janeiro. He urgently wanted to part company with her for reasons he preferred to keep to himself. We had stopped over in Rio for a few days on our journey south. He was a confident young man who prided himself in his ability to charm the ladies. He even boasted that he had been married briefly to a beauty queen, but he had no photographs to substantiate the story. Runner, the base plumber, was a loud, abrasive Welsh party animal. Bobby, the base electrician was boyish-faced, immature and tiresome. The two had become inseparable and were the mainstay of the bar and perpetrators of most drinking sessions. Ambrose kept up with them during their long drinking sessions but never really became a part of their elite group. They consistently gave other base members a bad time. I tried to be friendly towards them, but it was difficult living so close to people that you did not get on with, who continually irritated me like a nagging thorn. It was easier to get an early night than put up with their quibbling, bitching and alcohol-filled nonsense. This was the hard part of living in Antarctica.

Mike and Andy took the news badly. They were both very frustrated with BAS travel restrictions even though the rules made good sense. What they really wanted was to be on an expedition, not a job. Our thwarted attempt at Mount Peary added to their frustrations, and it was a silent threesome who made their long way back down the glacier to the dinghies and the long boat trip to Petermann island to attend to Runner. We arrived there late into the night. Mike diagnosed Runner as having nothing more than a bad cold, certainly caught from one of our many visitors in recent weeks.

Like all BAS doctors, Mike was expected to undertake a medical research project while on base. His project involved taping sensors to various parts of our anatomy and sticking our heads in a bucket of icy water and monitoring how long we could stand it. We breathed through a snorkel tube. In my case it was not for very long. Whatever he hoped to achieve I never knew. But I did know that he had little confidence that there was academic value in what he was doing. As a doctor, his medical functions on base were minimal. In fact, doctors on BAS bases are used as "gash-hands" for the greater part of the time. They help out with general chores around the base. Some BAS doctors accepted this, but others resented it. Mike was of the latter category.

We were almost at the end of summer. The Petermann incident was the last straw for Mike. He sent two telexes; one to his girlfriend read, "See you under the post office tower in Quito." The other to BAS read, "I resign."

Mike, however, did manage to get off base once more before he left. He returned to Petermann with Bobby and others to visit the French and say goodbye. Like me, he had the greatest respect for the achievements of the crew of Kim. The Bransfield's final call was drawing close. I helped his team load the dinghies and watched them disappear from view behind Grotto Island. I was always deeply envious of people getting off base, but I had plans for much more travel after the ship's final call.

I went up to the bar and joined Runner for a Gin and Tonic. Without Bobby's presence I got on better with him. We joked and talked. But before long the bottle was empty, so I went for a replacement from our prolific stock. We had so much of the stuff we even used it to clean bathroom mirrors and windows around the base! It was Sunday afternoon, normally a quiet time on base. Others joined in and, before long, more bottles were emptied. What followed was more like a bad dream. Even now I find it hard to recollect the exact sequence of events. I must have passed out because I only remember looking around the room and seeing bodies everywhere, as if someone had throw a stun grenade into the bar. It was surreal and bizarre, as if some mysterious illness had stuck everyone down — the gin I guessed. Then, after another period blanked from my memory, I found myself outside in the snow. There was another period of memory loss. Then I walked back into the base and saw at least ten people in the bathroom holding Runner's arm under a tap. Blood was spurting from huge tears in the flesh of his left hand. I looked on in amazement, not realising the seriousness of the situation. The doctor was away. Mike had left me in charge of his surgery "just in case!"

"Len, do something," they cried, the blood staining the walls and floor. My head spun, but the effect of alcohol was slightly diminished. I staggered off to the surgery room and opened Mike's cupboards. I tried to focus on the equipment while my mind raced over the options: injections, tablets, stitches, x-rays, bandages. There were rows of trays, scissors and funny tweezer-looking things. There were bedpans, neck braces, splints, plasters, needles and rows and rows of drugs. I focused on the drugs.

"Morphine, he needs morphine," I thought to myself.

I tore open a travel first aid kit and took out an ampoule, syringe and needle. Somehow, I assembled the syringe and filled it with the clear venomous-looking liquid. I staggered back down the corridor with the needle held high to avoid the liquid running out and onto the floor. I remembered to squeeze the air from the syringe. When Runner saw me enter the bathroom with the syringe held high he screamed.

"No! No! No!" He struggled violently, but the pack held him down.

"Inject him!" they shouted in unison, looking at me expectantly.

I stood in the doorway, undecided.

"Nooooooo!" screamed Runner.

"Inject him!" they shouted again, even louder as more of Runner's blood splattered up the bathroom wall.

I hesitated. I could barely focus on the circus before me. Then I moved forward. The throng held their breath. Runner was too terrified to scream. I plunged the needle into an arm, hopefully Runner's arm, one of many in the blood-filled sink. Runner collapsed, quiet and as meek as a lamb. I was not sure if it was from shock or the injection.

"Fuck. What have I done?" I thought and could hear the others thinking the same.

I had my doubts as to the wisdom of my actions. I started to bandage the wounds, but the blood kept coming through the bandages. I placed bandage upon bandage until there was a ball of bandages the size of a football covering his hand and I could no longer see the blood. Runner had ripped his hand open on the metal-plated cladding that partly lined the outside walls of the thirty-year-old base. Incomplete cladding that had dangerously sharp edges. Runner, like me, had been outside during the gin session. He had fallen to the ground from the effect of the gin and shredded his hand in the process.

We posted guards to monitor him during the night.

"If there's any change in his condition, call me," I said, stumbling off to be sick elsewhere and then to bed.

When I woke in the morning, I was filled with remorse and fearful memories of the night before. Someone was banging rocks against my head. I went back to the surgery room, but Runner was out. Ambrose had not surfaced.

"Petermann, Petermann, Faraday, over," I called and broke the news to Mike.

He was not pleased. His trips away from base had been doomed to failure. But he realised the urgency and returned immediately.

Runner eventually came to and was remarkably happy.

"Shit man!" was all he said for a long time, over and over again with a big grin. "That was some trip."

Summer was soon over, and it was time for those not staying the winter to leave. Despite the many drinking sessions and excursions, we had managed to achieve our work programme. The Bransfield made her final call, and some old friends were on board.

"I'm gonna walk to the South Pole next year," stated Bob Swan proudly, after his short summer season at Rothera painting and decorating.

"Yeah, Bob, and I'm gonna fly to the moon," I thought. I'd heard how he spent most of his time at Rothera trudging around base pulling a sledge practising for the big event.

But, Antarctica is vast. It's a big continent that makes you think big. And I had time to think while the Bransfield made her return trip to England.

I felt alone in a land of extremes — extreme weather, extreme size, extreme ideas and extreme drinking.

4

The fifteen of us that remained sat together in the bar, each with his own thoughts about the nine months ahead before the return of the Bransfield. Chris Jeffes had been appointed Base Commander (BC) for the winter. We had nicknamed him Joffs, and he had called the meeting. Joffs looked a young John Denver in every respect, down to his glasses and the shinning, well-placed teeth behind a wide mouth. He only lacked Denver's music ability. He was a likeable person with a huge task ahead as boss. BC was an envious, privileged position. But the winter ahead did not promise to be easy, and his Cambridge honours degree in agriculture was not likely to help. He shuffled nervously.

"Right, shut up you fuckers," he started the meeting, immediately identifying his style of management. "Item one is gash."

Gash was a hated chore. The daily gashman was nominated by rotation. The duties included cleaning the toilets, bar and dinning room, setting the tables at meal times and washing the dishes. It came around all too soon.

"I do too many Saturdays," complained Ian. "I've done three in the last fucking two months. Why?"

Ian Davies was a burly carpenter who looked distinctly Norwegian with his bushy, blonde beard, thickset face and hair parted neatly at one side. But he was, in fact, English. Ian found it difficult to befriend anyone in particular. His only ambition from day one at Faraday was to get the two-and-a-half-year trip over and done with and to get the hell out of there. But he had a long time to go! As soon as he arrived on base, he built himself a "goodies box" for his personal effects ready for the journey home. He continually redesigned the box over the next two and a half years. Packing became an obsession with him, and he talked about little else.

"I'll look into it," replied Joffs, unconvincingly.

"Cunt," whispered Ian so that anyone but Joffs could hear and poked his middle finger in the air. Ian did not have a great deal of patience with Joffs, or with anyone or anything else for that matter.

"Gash," Joffs continued, "I will make up the daily rota for a month in advance."

Andy gave one of the deep "gwaff, gwaff" noises to add to the hubbub of non-interested meeting members. Runner and Bobby were leading the bar-brigade. I wondered if their winter stock of beer would last.

"What about Pint?" shouted Bobby. "Why shouldn't the fucking cook do gash?" He smirked at Pint. "Up yer ass," he mouthed at Pint, grinning from ear to ear. Gerraint "Pint" Hughes was Welsh and the Faraday cook, a professional pastry chef with the thankless task of keeping us fed. He always came under criticism, which he took badly. "Whale meet again, don't know where, don't know when … " often sung, causing Pint to throw a tantrum and sink himself into a bottle of something strong.

Pint was a thin, slight nervous person with piercing eyes and narrow mouth. He was better suited to the confines of a Welsh bar than to enduring the rigours of Antarctica. He was happy indoors and like a fish out of water on those few occasions when he ventured outdoors. But Pint was popular. He worked long hours and sank himself into alcohol, cigarettes and a book every Sunday. It was his only free time. He said nothing and just grinned at Bobby.

"Silence for fuck's sake," screamed Joffs, ignoring Booby's outburst. He was losing control. "Scrubouts," he said, moving on to the next item. The crowd grew noisier, and more alcohol was consumed. And so the meeting progressed from item to item with Joffs trying to get consensus of opinion on routine jobs like scrubouts, snow blocking and Sunday-cook. Even film nights, the only entertainment evening, was on the agenda. The hard core of drinkers gathered round the bar and became more and more raucous.

"Doctor," said Joffs, the last item on his impromptu agenda. He was clearly weary of his new role as BC.

"We don't have one. He fucked off and left us," someone offered.

I wondered if Mike's ears twitched aboard the Bransfield on his way to his date in Quito.

"Yeah, yeah, clever ass. We fucking need one don't we? Who's gonna do it?"

There was near order among the FIDS. We all looked at each other. Don twitched enthusiastically, obviously considering the prospect of becoming a doctor met-man. Ambrose smiled sadistically. There was no way that any of them was going to stick needles into my arm or administer dangerous drugs to my stomach, I thought.

"I'll do it!" said Andy, as he kicked his legs into the air and simulated an injection into his rear. "I'll inject yer bums, gwaff, gwaff."

Sometimes I hated that cunt. He could be so fucking annoying, and he did it on purpose.

"Self service," suggested Bobby. "If you need drugs, just help yourself ha, ha, ha ... but don't let Runner in there!"

"Fuck off Banner. Hey, Bobby, how about a rave in the surgery," shouted Runner to a chorus of laughter.

"Shut the fuck up all of you. We need someone to take on the job of medic," shouted Joffs.

Oh shit, I thought. This is a fucking madhouse. I'm locked in here for the winter with fourteen fucking weirdoes! "I'll do it for fuck sake," I announced less than enthusiastically. I wondered what bits of bloody flesh and weeping penises would be brought my way during the winter. But I was the oldest and perhaps the best of a bad bunch. The sea was about to freeze over, barring any way in or out of Faraday. Dr. Len Airey would have to cope with whatever illness the "weirdoes" brought upon themselves. I remembered reading one of the old base reports. There had been an attempt some years earlier to land a light aircraft close to the base and evacuate the cook, who was extremely ill. The aircraft managed to land but, unfortunately, hit an iceberg on takeoff and was destroyed. The cook and crew managed to survive the crash, but the cook later died in a South American hospital from his illness.

I moved from my tent into the base. If there was one thing that I hated, that was sharing a room. The base had eight tiny bedrooms with two bunks per room. Joffs elected to have a room to himself, which meant the rest of us had to share. I was having none of it; I moved into an attic space above the radio room. But I did have space on base, the Beastie room and now my new acquisition, the surgery room.

I kept the surgery door under lock and key. Already there were large amounts of Pethidine and Diconal missing. And, according to the little information I had, these were desirable drugs for undesirables — junkie material. I looked at my new toys: x-ray machines, dental equipment, an anesthatiser, a couch, stretcher, bed pots, disinfecting equipment, crutches and lots and lots of little pots of drugs.

"I'm going deaf," said Tim, my first patient.

"What?" I replied.

"I'm going..." but stopped when he saw me laughing.

Tim was the chief met-man and was in his second winter at Faraday. He was a slight, popular person who kept himself to himself. His straight moustache almost covered the breadth of his face. He reminded me of Groucho Marx, without the cigar. He was always extremely polite, and I never saw him cross or depressed, a remarkable feat considering the circumstances. He had mastered the art of living and working in Antarctica and was extremely patient with the new Doc.

Among the array of medical tools I found a suitable-looking instrument which was obviously designed for looking into small dark orifices as it provided both illumination and magnification. I poked it into Tim's ear and peered inside. The first thing that occurred to me was how uncomfortable I felt so close to another man, a sensation I felt when dentists peered into my mouth. I saw a large bung of brown wax deep in his ear.

"You're full of shit, Tim. I'm going to have to syringe your ears," I guessed.

I'd heard about people having their ears syringed, but I had no idea how to do it. There were doctors at the other BAS bases: Rothera to the south, Signey and Grytviken on the sub-Antarctic islands, and Halley on an ice shelf, the most southerly of all BAS bases. Each base had its specific scientific programme. I had Ambrose make a radio call to Rothera, and I made arrangements with their doctor for a daily medical discussion of my patients. We started with Tim.

That evening Tim sat trustingly in my surgery room as I filled an enormous syringe with warm water. Tilting his head to one side, I pumped the liquid deep into his ear.

"How you doing, Tim" I asked, pumping as fast as I dared. Great lumps of wax came out with the water, which I collected in a tray that fitted around his neck and could have been designed for the purpose. I felt sick.

"Giddy," he complained. "I think I'm going to fall over."

The water was affecting his sense of balance. I'd had enough, anyway.

"OK, Tim," I said in a low soothing tone, like doctors do. "Let's have another go tomorrow to get the rest out."

Poor Tim, just a victim of circumstances, saddled with a quack at the bottom of the world.

I handed him a paper towel to dry his ear, as a doctor would have done.

5

"What's new, Ambrose?" someone asked, a frequent plea for something new to talk about at meal times. It was a difficult time for all of us; the monotony at times was hard to bear. Ambrose rarely volunteered information even though he listened to all the base conversations and the world news. He regularly contacted people on the Falkland Islands and Hams around the world. It was a sort of game with him, to keep news to himself when he knew that we were desperate for something new to talk about.

"Nuffin much," he grinned as always when he knew he was the centre of attention. Ambrose liked being the centre of attention. "Hm, a BAS Twin Otter crashed yesterday at Rothera. Nobody was injured. But the plane is bust, so they are going to crate it up and ship it out next year for repair."

BAS had two Twin Otter aircraft used in the summer to ferry geologists and glaciologists deep into Antarctica.

"Hm, the Biscoe was towed back to South America for repairs. But in the end they decided that she could slowly steam her way back home, and they will repair it there. Something wrong with the propeller I think. Hm, the Bransfield has picked up an accused murderer from the Falkland Islands and is taking him back to the UK for trial. Nuffin else that I can think of. Nuffin much at all."

It was nothing to Ambrose, but big news to us. The failure on the Biscoe, BAS' second Antarctic vessel, would seriously disrupt their scientific programme. These snippets of information fed rumours. Rumours were perpetuated on purpose by some to create uncertainty. Idle conversation for the hell of it often chipped away at base morale.

It was Easter, and we were in the transition period between "summer travel" by dinghy and "winter travel" over sea ice. A thin film of ice on the sea made travel by dinghy impossible, but the ice was too thin to walk across. It was a difficult time for us while we were confined to the tiny island, less than one square kilometre and only sixty-five metres at its highest point. Until the sea froze over with a thick bed of ice, we were stranded there. Air temperatures rarely dropped much below freezing during these transient months, even though the sun was setting longer as winter approached. Lower air temperatures and a period free of storms was essential before the sea ice could form.

In preparation for winter travel and to encourage some outside activity, I started some mountaineering training and repeated the emergency training course we all attended with BAS in Derbyshire — only this time on ice. Base morale was noticeably different when people got out and away from the continual banter and backbiting. But we were only at the beginning of our winter. It was only a month since the Bransfield had left. The tension between some base members was growing. Some formed small groups of buddies. Stronger characters continually picked on weaker ones. The worst time of day was meal time. Each had his place at the dining room table. Groups of two or three would throw cutting remarks across the table to whomever they thought it would irritate the most. The worst thing to do was to react. Even the slightest comment could result in a severe mental beating. At first I likened it to schoolchildren's behaviour. But it was worse than that, malicious, cruel and damaging. Behaviour expected of a group of wild animals taken from their habitat and thrown together in cages. That's what it felt like. Tension between base members reached a pinnacle during bad weather, when storms lashed outside and the cage door was locked. Storms would last for days, sometime weeks. The animals would grow more and more restless. They often turned on themselves, the ones they confided in. This was more than hurtful, it was unbearable — dog eat dog. If an owner treated his dogs like this, he would have been thrown behind bars! The hurt animal would hide and sulk, often for days. Only a break in the weather would break the cycle.

Working hard and long hours alleviated the boredom. We trained one of the others as a stand-in to do our work when the time came to be off base on a "jolly" — a recreational field trip. Barry, my fellow Ionosphericist, took care of my work. Barry was a serious, politically-correct, well liked individual who was sick of base life. He'd had enough, and only valour kept him from boarding the Bransfield on her last call. All he wanted was to get home and go through with the marriage he and his girl-friend had planned for so long. Barry had learned the art of survival from the animals — say nothing and, when it got too much, walk away. But inside, he hurt.

Base routine was monotonous, but necessary. Every night at five-o'clock, whatever the weather, we gathered in front of the base to cut blocks of hard packed snow for fresh water. Sometimes it was the highlight of the day — the only time we were outside in the fresh Antarctic air. Someone would hack at a fresh mound of snow, trying to release tension. Ian or Andy would do it to vent a grudge. A line was formed, and blocks were passed down. At the front of the base they were piled ready for the gashman to periodically drop them down a chute that led into a heated water tank. When snow was not available, usually during the summer months, we towed chunks of glacier ice ashore and split them up with ice axes and hammers. Even so, there was always a shortage of water on base, and showers were restricted to once a week. I hated this restriction and missed having a hot shower at the beginning and end of each day.

Everyone loathed gash. It was done in strict rotation, and some did it better than others.

"Where's the fucking gashman? The cunt hasn't set the tables, mixed the milk — not even filled the fucking salt sellers. Ambrose, where the fuck are you, you lazy cunt!" It was an onerous but necessary task. At least it was a break from the normal routine, a marker.

"Only twenty-five gashes 'til the Brany gets back!" was one of Joffs favourites.

Scrubout was a weekly routine, a Saturday morning activity in which everyone was given a task. The whole base was cleaned, including workshops. Scrubout marked the end of the work week. It ended at lunchtime, and lunch was served in the bar. The drinking started. The afternoon was time to relax, take the only shower of the week and get ready for Saturday night when the animals would party!

The tradition on BAS bases was to dress up for Saturday night dinner, or at least put on something other than FID issue, such as a one-piece, bright red, combination long johns and vest. Some, however, preferred a more traditional collar and tie, or even a suit. Most made an effort to maintain tradition. But there were those who refused to join in and turned up in their everyday work clothes. This was all part of the suffering in the living together. It was the unwillingness, or lack of ability, to work as a team. It was a reflection on their personality. The expectations of the cook on Saturday nights were high, and Pint delivered without fail. Cocktails were served in the bar before dinner, the candles were lit, music was selected and the gashman and assistant waiter served a five-course meal. There was something eerie or surreal about Saturday nights. Fifteen men in Antarctica sat in silence around a candle-lit table sipping Mateus Rose or Champagne Moet, eating king prawn provocale followed by roast baron of beef. There was always tension at the table, waiting for one of the animals to start something. It was an unwritten law that there was a truce on Saturday nights. But it created an uncomfortable atmosphere that occasionally exploded. The tension ended when the signal was given to wash up. This was a joint effort before retiring to the bar for the inevitable heavy drinking session to put the world problems to right. Some preferred to avoid the bar and retire early to avoid the animals lashing at the bars of their cages.

Sunday night was film night. The gashman was privileged to choose the film, but not without pressure from the others. With just one film per week, apart from special film nights such as birthdays, it was one of the highlights of the week, particularly if the film was any good. If not, there was all hell to pay. BAS got the blame. The Sunday cook was expected to prepare "film goodies," and it was the only day of the week we had crisps and peanuts — a real treat! The one pornographic film we possessed lost its novelty after watching Rachael dress, undress, smile and take her smile back at a variety of speeds. Watching her dress was no more erotic than watching her undress when "Get 'em on!" replaced "Get 'em off!"

It was six months since I sailed from Southampton. Most of the wildlife had gone north to escape the winter, and only the FIDS and Paddies remained. The Sheathbills (or Paddies as they are known) stay in Antarctica throughout the winter, living off the kitchen waste and human excrement dumped into the sea. In late May the skies cleared in the permanent Antarctic night. The air temperature dropped causing the sea to begin its winter freeze. The landscape slowly took on its winter coat as sea and land became one. There was an excited atmosphere on base as most of us looked forward to travel without the hindrance of seawater. Like a curtain at the beginning of the next act, the shadow over us began to lift. The bridge to the lands beyond was forming.

The creeks between the Faraday islands partly froze. I was about to ski across Stella Creek to the old Wordie base on one of my regular visits when I spotted Andy at the door of the hut wearing just a blanket. A hole in the ice marked the end of his ski tracks where the ice had broken under him. He had lost both skis in the process. His tracks indicated that he had crawled across the wafer thin ice to reach the safety of Wordie hut. If he had not reached Wordie within three or four minutes, he would have succumbed to the cold and died. The accident was a stark reminder of the danger we faced while crossing the sea ice. But the ice thickened rapidly over the next few weeks and was soon four or five inches thick — thick enough to support our weight. We always travelled on skis, probing the ice in front of us with a bog chisel, a sharp metal spike on a long wooden pole. Each evening we discussed the advance of the winter ice. Groups of three or four were planning the logistics of their winter travel, some more ambitiously than others.

While waiting for winter travel to commence, I desperately needed something to occupy my time. What was missing on base, I decided, was a sauna! Between the main base and the generator shed was the old boat shed, which was used to house our four large walk-in freezers and some general storage. One of the freezers was old and no longer used, so I procured it for the Faraday sauna. The freezer's heavily insulated walls were ideal for the purpose. Ian cut up as much wood as he could spare, and I completely lined the inside of the freezer with strips of pine. I fitted one of the old base windows into the door and modified the lock so that it could not be locked from the inside. Ian helped me furnish the inside with slated benches, and Bobby installed a

powerful electric heater to get the freezer up to sauna temperature. The finished product was truly impressive; it was a great
success. We had the inevitable inauguration party. Thereafter a
Saturday night sauna with a roll in the snow became a part of
base routine.

One of the greatest hazards on base was the risk of fire. The
buildings were constructed of wood, dried brittle in the humid-
ity-free climate. We made a rotation for fire-watch duty.
Fire-watch was very popular. The duty person had the whole
base to himself. Every night for a week that person watched
while the rest slept. It was a welcome break from the normal routine and a time to be alone. Many, including myself, would have
done permanent fire-watch given half the chance.

We assumed crime on Faraday to be non-existent until we
discovered a chocolate thief among us. Our stockpile was rapidly dwindling, causing more tension than the problem war-
ranted. Pint decided to give out a monthly chocolate ration in
order to keep the peace. Huge piles of Cadbury's Walnut, Mars
Bars and other mouth-watering names were handed out each
month. It was far more chocolate than I really wanted to eat. The
result was that I accumulated a massive stockpile of chocolate
during the winter months.

Our elation at the arrival of the sea ice was short lived. The air
temperature rose to plus seven, gale-force winds lashed the
base, and the newly formed sea ice broke up. There was open
water all the way from Faraday to the mainland. We were forced
to stay indoors. Once again we were trapped in the cage, and the
tension between base members rose to an all time high. Faraday
had returned to being just a bleak wind tunnel. The gales continued for weeks.

My medical responsibilities kept me busy during the storm. I
was learning all the time and gaining in confidence as more people came to me to cure their ills. Syringing ears became popular
after my success with Tim, and I went on to fill teeth, treat

Trench Mouth — whatever that is — cure ear infections, test urine and take x-rays. I was even expected to cure insomnia and depression, and to council other personal problems! My radio schedules with the Rothera doctor gave me a chance to chat with someone different. Steve Tait, who was sheltered in a tent somewhere on the Antarctic plateau, joined in one night.

"How's it going, Steve?" I asked. I remembered a particular game of football we had played in our climbing boots while on the Derbyshire field-training course with BAS. We had great fun during the course, bonding as a team, all of us ready for the adventure ahead in Antarctica.

"I'm on a jolly with John Anderson, Bob Atkinson and Nigel Hadley," he said. "A storm is making it impossible for us to move from our tents and get back to base."

"Can't be a lot to do for weeks on end stuck in a tent," I said rather stupidly, but not being able to think of anything else to say.

"No," he replied quietly.

I thought of John laying alongside Steve in his sleeping bag in the confines of the tent, and I chuckled to myself. I thought of him trying to play football in his huge climbing boots. John ran a climbing shop in Inverness before joining BAS. His record of amazing climbing feats spoke for itself. But he did not look the part, more a timid, shy person — an office worker with a great sense of humour. Bob, the Rothera cook, on the other hand, had no mountaineering experience. He had been terrified of flying in one of the BAS planes to get to Rothera. He could hardly speak of it through his stammer.

I dedicated more time to using the radio equipment so that I could relieve Ambrose for time off base when the travel season started. I was already fluent in Morse Code, and my operating skills were improving rapidly by hamming as much as I could — or rather, as much as Ambrose would allow me. It was not long before I took over one radio "sched" per week. I transmitted the met-man's daily weather report in Morse to Frei, a Chilean base at the northern end of the Antarctic Peninsula, and the morning telex schedule to Cable and Wireless in Port Stanley.

We received news that the Bransfield had arrived back in Southampton. May was coming to a close, but the storms raged on. We were now resigned to not travelling until after mid-winter. Then the sun would return for the Antarctic spring, bringing longer days.

We arranged a Saturday night darts match against Palmer station, an American base north of Faraday. They were our closest neighbours, although it was not possible to visit them. We each had our own darts board, and a commentator transmitted the play and score over the radio. It relied on a great deal of honesty from both sides!

"Triple twenty ... ten ... and bulls eye ... one hundred and treeeeenty!" they shouted over the radio to a chorus of background whoops and cheers.

We threw our darts. "One hundred and twenty!" we responded in all honesty. We had some well-practised players. Roars of laughter and cheers came over the radio from the opposition. The stakes were two barrels of beer. But delivery was a problem.

"Legs eleven," their next throw against a background of boos.

We played on into the Antarctic night.
Who's to know when the game is over,
and the storm abates.

6

The sound of voices from the radio below woke me. Only the hands of the clock penetrated the darkness, but I was in no condition to focus on them. I turned over in my sleeping bag and rolled off the mattress onto the wooden floor in search of something to drink. It was Sunday morning; last night was one of those nights I preferred to forget. All hell was let loose in my head. The windowless attic where I slept was hot and stuffy. My hand located a familiar pile of soft drinks stored in the corner. I pulled out a can from the pile, rolled back onto the mattress and swigged at the warm, fizzy liquid. It was a coke. I would have preferred orange. But my throat was as dry as a vulture's armpit, and anything would do to re-hydrate me and take away the taste of alcohol. For all I knew, or cared, it was mid-day.

I strained to hear what was being said below. The reception improved slightly, and I recognised the voices. Mouse, the Rothera Base BC, was talking to Steve. He was still camped somewhere high on a glacier above Rothera. Mark Lewis earned the nickname Mouse two years before when, in a state of inebriation, he staggered onto the bridge of the Bransfield. It was docked in Rio de Janeiro. Mouse was wearing a set of Mickey Mouse ears he had brought with him on the voyage south form Southampton.

"I'm Mouse," he was reported to have slurred. "Where the fuck's Big Ears?"

Apparently, the Captain took it all in good spirit and watched bemused as Mouse staggered off in search of his mate. What is not clear is if Big Ears was a figment of Mouse's pickled imagination or there really was someone else in a similar state of inebriation and disguise, either looking for or hiding from Mouse.

Storms had swept the Antarctic Peninsula for more than six weeks. They had torn at the walls of our tiny wooden hut in an excited fervour and whistled through the aerials – the same aerials that captured the voices on the radio. Finally the storm had abated. The walls of my attic room were still and silent. I tried to remember for how long Steve, John, Bob and Nigel had been trapped in their tents, waiting for the storms to end and allowing them to return to Rothera. Each morning and evening I had listened to them report back to base. Each day I felt their frustration and boredom while pinned down by the freezing, murderous torment. Nothing would have tempted them from their precarious refuge unless it threatened their very existence — a torn tent, a loose guy or the threat of being buried by drifting snow. Just two nights ago I listened to how they had suspended themselves from the apex of the tent to keep it from lifting in the wind, leaving them to freeze to death without shelter.

I focused on the alarm; it was just 7 a.m. By now the sun would be on the horizon casting shadows of the great icebergs carved from the Wiggins and Bussey glaciers across the partially frozen sea. Antarctica was desolate at this time of year — no ships, no planes, just tiny populations on remote stations. There was no way in or out of Faraday. I was imprisoned until

Antarctica was ready to release me. The isolation was complete, unimaginably remote and void of any interruption from the world I had left months before. I felt wonderfully alone, in a coffin. It would be two and a half years before the lid would open and release me and return me to society. I had time to reflect on where I wanted my life to go. After Antarctica I would start again, a new beginning. But first I needed to cleanse my body of the alcohol from the night before. I couldn't remember who won the darts match; but, then, it didn't really matter.

I sipped at my coke and thought about the day ahead. I needed to get out; I needed exercise after being stuck on base for so long during the storm. I knew that great mounds of soft snow would have been dumped around the base by the swirling wind. Skiing anywhere would be hard work. I wondered if the sky was clear. If it were, there would be a good day on base. The animals would be tamed. There would be laughter and animosities forgotten.

My hand searched the wall above my head for the light switch. A dull red glow illuminated the attic. The jeans and shirt I wore for the darts match the previous night were strewn across the floor. I reached into a cardboard box with Heinz Baked Beans printed across the side and pulled out a clean pair of moleskin trousers, a thick cotton vest and a pair of woollen socks. I dressed horizontally because, even at its highest point, the ceiling was so low that I could barely kneel. The colours had run in the wash, and almost everything I wore was the same dull grey-blue colour. The base had an iron, but it was rarely used. My books, cassettes and other small personal effects were neatly stacked next to the soft drinks. A case of malt whiskey, a case of Three Nuns dry white wine and an assortment of other drinks almost filled the remainder of the attic floor. Even though it was uncomfortable, I still preferred the privacy of the attic to sharing a bunkroom.

I opened a hatch in the floor and climbed the short vertical ladder down into the main corridor. I entered the radio room. Ambrose was just completing his morning "scheds" and would soon be back in bed.

"Hi, Ambrose," I replied in a dull tone through my hangover. I knew his head would be worse than mine. Ambrose was always one of the last to leave the bar on Saturday nights. "Steve's spoke to Mouse?"

"We've pitched the tent close to the crevasse and will stay here until someone arrives."

Steve spoke in a low, controlled voice. I could visualise him lying in his pyramid tent. It was the kind that Scott used on his epic journey to the South Pole nearly seventy years before — a journey from which Scott and his companions never returned.

"We'll be there in about two hours," replied Mouse.

"Where are they. And why is Mouse sending someone out to get them?" I asked Ambrose as he fiddled with the radio.

"Dunno," he replied, disinterested.

Ambrose sometimes had a matter-of-fact way about him, and he was obviously not in the mood for idle chat.

"Perhaps their skidoo broke down. Maybe they should have used the dogs!" I said, but dropped the subject when I got no response from Ambrose.

I left Ambrose to complete his "sched" and made my way down the chilly corridor to the dinning room for breakfast. It was deserted. Most people were still in bed.

The bright Formica tables, matching chairs, walls and ceiling resembled a school dinning room. It was not as I had imagined an Antarctic research station. I had expected a hut filled with the stench of seal blubber, a roaring coke fire, cramped living conditions and everyone dressed in fur-lined jackets and boots. But that was not to be.

I sat facing a door that led through to the well-stocked bar. Last winter's carpenter had built an extraordinary amount of detail into the room. The teak surrounds and matching high stools would have been well placed in most hotels. The bar was littered with empty and part-empty bottles and glasses, bringing back memories of the night before and the heated discussions that always drove me to bed earlier than most. Darts were lying on the floor as if the last thrower failed to reach the board. I closed the door in order to eat my breakfast without the stench of stale cigarettes and spilt alcohol.

After breakfast I made my way back down the empty corridor towards my workroom. I passed the radio room. Ambrose was still listening in to Rothera. He cursed my Beastie, as it scanned the ionosphere. It caused severe interference on his radio, cutting out Mouse's conversation with Steve for a few seconds.

"How are they doing?" I asked.

"Hm," was all I got out of him.

The weather was good — clear blue skies. It was a day for the hill and skiing. By mid-day most people were up, and most with hangovers. Pint had the day off; this was the down side of Sundays. It was our turn to cook, and today's lunch was well down on the popularity rating, probably as close to zero as one could get.

"Soup?" asked Ambrose, as if it were some exotic dish we had never heard of.

"What the fuck is this, Ambrose? You're an idle cunt!" said Runner, poking the fish head looking back at him from the murky liquid.

Barry took Runner's word for it and turned to the fridge to see what Pint had left from the previous day, but for once nobody cared. There was a sense of urgency to get the meal over and enjoy the sunshine while it lasted.

Few people stayed on base in the afternoon. There was a mass exodus to enjoy the brilliant sunshine and downhill skiing on Woozle Hill. Woozle may have been only sixty-five metres above sea level, but skiing down its slopes in the deep powder snow was exhilarating. We were towed back to its summit at kamikaze speeds by a skidoo driven by Don. Andy was the only proficient skier among us. The rest of us struggled in the deep powder, taking our tumbles in the snow like six-year-olds. Exhausted but happy, we headed back to base in the early evening in time for snow blocking.

As usual we congregated in the bar for a few drinks before dinner. The talk was of travel for a change. Finally, would the sea ice form and stay? It was film night, and we had had the best day in weeks. Ambrose was back in the kitchen, and it was not long before the gashman summoned us from the bar.

"Come and get it!" called Ambrose, and added in a rather low and smirking voice, "If you must. I've had a really busy day." He was grinning wider than ever as he pulled his effort from the oven. Our fears were justified.

"Rat shit."

"Cunt."

"I can't eat this ... donkey spew ... "

"Fuck you, Ambrose."

It was not possible to be complimentary. Most just served it onto their plates, secretly thankful that this was one meal that was not going to put the pounds on. Ian stormed out, slamming the door behind him. Barry opened the fridge without saying a word.

Joffs stood up to make an announcement. He was nervous, but he was always nervous. He hated speaking in public. He read aloud a message from the Director of BAS. As he read, a chill swept through the base. "John Anderson and Bob Atkinson were killed yesterday while trying to get back to Rothera. They had been on a field trip and were laid up in their tents for many weeks during violent storms. While returning, they drove over a snow bridge covering a huge crevasse. The bridge collapsed. They both fell into the crevasse along with their skidoo. Steve

Taite managed to climb down to them. He found John Anderson on a ledge still alive, but he died shortly thereafter. There was no sign of Bob Atkinson. He is presumed to have died instantly at the bottom of the crevasse. Steve Taite and Nigel Hadley were with John and Bob. Mark Lewis has sent a rescue party to assist them back to base. All our heartfelt sympathies have gone out to the families of John and Bob."

Joffs sat down, and we ate the rat shit and donkey spew in silence.

For all of us it was more than a job.
For some, it was more than it was worth.

The end of May brought clear skies and beautiful sunshine. My sense of smell was acute in the pollution-free environment. The sweet, distinct aroma of sun cream filled the air and was accompanied by well tanned, happy faces as we skied down from the top of Woozle hill. The weather had broken for the better, and differences were forgotten, shelved for another stormy day.

I found new ways to pass the time now that the weather had improved. I'd found a small drogue parachute in the old boat shed. I skied out onto the sea ice in a strong breeze, opened the

chute and held on to the handles as the wind filled the canopy. I was propelled along the ice at breath-taking speeds ... they were happy days, fulfilling the reason for being in Antarctica. They were days worth the pain of incarceration, days when I thought I could stay in Antarctica forever.

The weather stabilised and temperatures fell to twenty degrees below zero. This caused rapid freezing of the sea. We talked constantly of travel. I skied out into Penola Straight—the deep water channels that separated Faraday from the mainland. The sea ice was smooth and shiny, like an ice-rink, but wafer thin. It was just two or three centimetres thick in places. When I saw penguins leaping into open water just in front of me, I realised that I was in danger. My bog chisel pierced easily through the ice in front of me. Had the ice broken under me, it would have been impossible for me to climb back onto the thin ice. The sea ice grew thicker each day. Eventually a thick covering of fresh snow gave the ice the thickness and strength required to travel across it safely. Before long there was hardly a patch of open water to be seen. The time for winter travel had arrived.

With Don and Runner, I reached Petermann hut early in June. The Kim was locked into thick sea ice. I was surprised that they had left the yacht in the ice rather than dragging it out of the water. The hull could have been crushed by pressure from the ice. Michelle was alone. Both he and the hut stank from the rancid seal fat they used for cooking and heating. The old Argentine base was a mess, black and dirty. There were clothes, parts from the boat, dirty pots and pans, and bits of food everywhere. Daniel, Bruno and Claude were out hunting for food. The state of the hut must have resembled how people lived in Antarctica before the all-encompassing and relatively luxurious bases were constructed. I still felt envious of their adventure, their freedom and their resilience to danger.

I left Don and Runner with Michelle and went in search of the others. I found them in the Lemaire Channel. This was the first time I had returned to the channel since arriving on the Bransfield. How different it was, now covered in ice and almost void of wildlife. The silence was complete and the beauty magnificent. The feeling of solitude, a tiny figure in a never-ending wilderness of ice, left a life-long impression on me. They stood next to a Leopard seal they had just shot. They'd seen it the day before eating a young Crabeater seal. They had already removed its head. Its massive jaws lay wide open, and its eyes stared into space. I felt sad that the magnificent beast had to die. We cut the carcass into manageable pieces, loaded it onto their sledge and hauled it back through the channel to Petermann. A pool of blood and intestine stained the otherwise lily-white snow. But somewhere, close bye, the Paddies would be watching and waiting.

It had been nearly three months since we had last seen the French, and there was a lot to talk about. We huddled around the smoking stove in the Petermann hut and prepared a meal of seal liver and rice. Thick black smoke from the burning blubber impregnated my clothes, skin, eyes, hair and nostrils; and I soon bore the same repugnant smell as the French. We exchanged news as we ate. I had brought wine. They were shocked by the accident at Rothera. They told us how they, too, had come close to losing their lives while sleeping on the yacht. During the night the sea ice moved, snapping a fitting on the hull and seawater poured into the yacht as they slept. The yacht filled to the level of their bunks. It was close to sinking. By chance, they awoke to discover the danger. Since that day, they had slept in the hut. It was less comfortable, but much safer. They told us how they had occupied their time during the summer by making gifts to take home. They used the bones and hides of seals and penguins that they had eaten. We talked and drank gin late into the night. Eventually the temperature in the hut dropped to an unbearable low, and we sought the warmth of our sleeping bags and a good night's sleep.

The next morning we visited the French's pet Emperor penguin. It was a young male, a metre tall and looking every bit as majestic as its name suggested. Far from home, it had taken a likeness to the hospitality of the French and accepted odd bits of food from them. It was not in the least bit perturbed by our presence. The young Emperor would not breed for at least another two years or more. He could live for more than twenty-five years if he managed to avoid his predators, the Leopard seals, Killer whales and French!

With Daniel and Michelle I skied across Penola Straight in a strong, cold wind to investigate a ramp to the foot of the glacier at Moot Point. The ramp provided a possible route to the base of Mount Shackleton, a peak I was keen to climb. This was the closest I had come to the Antarctic mountains. I felt excited by the prospect of the climb. The ramp was good, better than expected. I made a pact with the French to attempt the mountain within the next few days.

Daylight hours were increasingly short, just six hours a day. It was already getting late by the time we left the ramp. We hurried back across Penola Strait towards Faraday, arriving in the dark with plummeting temperatures. The others had travelled directly from Petermann and arrived shortly after us. The shower was a blessing after the stench of the hut, but that was only after one night. I imagined for the French that it was paradise! I had skied fifty kilometres in two days and could only briefly join in to the celebration party for the French before I collapsed into bed.

Forty knot winds, heavy snow and rising temperatures kept us indoors for the next few days. I was afraid that the sea ice would once again break up. The French joined in all of the base duties, helping out with the work wherever they could. They integrated as best they could, but there was a certain resentment by some over their presence on base. It was not the animals that resented the French. It was the silent few, those that only wanted to serve their time and offered nothing to base life. They saw any break in their routine as an annoyance, and they complained bitterly that the French were allowed to stay. But Joffs had the final word, and the French stayed. Personally, I found the whole thing disturbing. Their experience extended far beyond Antarctica. They had so much to share, and I wanted to hear every word. Their presence was also calming on base. The animals were much more subdued and rattled their cages less frequently. The silent few remained silent after their initial moaning session.

Birthdays were special days, and Ambrose's 21st birthday on the 4th of June was no exception. He spent most of the day drinking and was already well inebriated before his party began. In fact, he was positively obnoxious, and most people avoided him. Ambrose insisted on having a fancy dress birthday with the theme of babies' night, the only babies' night with a 21st birthday cake! Fifteen FIDS and four French sailors sat around the table wearing nappies and ribbons in their hair. Custard, chocolate cake, strawberry flan and whips covered the table. The nineteen drunken babies, many with bushy beards, sat wondering who was going to start it. The end result was inevitable, so I decided to begin. I picked up a large custard pie and pushed it firmly in Ambrose's face.

"Oh, fuck," he giggled, making no attempt to remove it.

The evening turned into chaos as food was flung across the tables, covering the dinning room walls, ceiling and floor — nineteen grown men behaving like babies. The animals loved it, and even the silent few joined in.

The clean-up operation was a lengthy one, taking us well past midnight. And we still found remnants of food from the party months later. The night ended in the usual heated bar discussions on inane topics — finally breaking down into full-blown quarrels. Eventually everyone went to their beds, with the exception of the hardened drinkers.

Two days later I left with Bobby, Runner and some of the French to attempt Mount Shackleton. Neither Bobby nor Runner had climbed before, and their lack of mountaineering experience was cause for concern. But they were adamant about wanting to attempt the mountain. We left at first light and hauled our laden sledges across the ten kilometres of excellent sea ice to the ramp at Moot Point. The journey was exhilarating and the weather perfect. Hauling a laden sledge across the frozen sea, skirting icebergs and stopping for well-earned rests was all I ever longed for in Antarctica. The ramp was steep and required the use of our Tirfor winches to haul the sledges to the top. We were faced with a maze of crevasses and towers of ice. Bruno and I picked our way through the seracs and gaping chasms which marked the end of the Wiggins Glacier. We were looking for a route through to the ice ramps above and a way up Shackleton — but it was impossible. There was no way through the tangle of ice, and we had to accept defeat. Beaten but not despondent, we lowered all the equipment back down to sea level and made camp for the night.

The aroma of French cuisine seal steaks drifted from our tent as we planned the following day's activities. With only five hours of daylight, the days were too short for making a serious attempt on the mountain. The sun barely rose above the horizon before it set again. And it was bitterly cold. We decided that Shackleton would have to wait until later in the winter. It was the right decision and did not take away from the splendour of our excursion into the mountains. Runner and Bobby were quietly pleased. They were not enjoying the hardships away from the comforts of base. I was quietly pleased because they were a liability in the mountains. It was better for all of us if they stayed in the bar. Instead of climbing the mountain, we decided to explore the southern coastline, investigating other ramps in the area that could provided access to the glaciers above.

The next morning we moved our camp south to Waddington Bay from where we would attempt to climb Mount Demaira. An easy-looking ridge of rock and ice reached up to the summit six hundred and fifty metres higher. It offered good views of the sea ice and mountains further south. Bobby and Runner preferred the relative comfort of the tent while Bruno, Claude and I made for the summit. It was bitterly cold with overcast skies. The contrast was poor, making it hard to discern the route ahead. We became covered in hoarfrost; our beards and clothes turned white. But as we climbed and the sun winked slightly higher above the horizon, the visibility improved. The scenery was spectacular. The sea was white and frozen solid to the horizon in every direction. Faraday was lost from view, somewhere distant in the white chaos. The ice cliffs dwarfed our tent, a prick of red far below. The freezing air burnt our lungs. Our heavy breathing was the only sound to penetrate the silence that surrounded us. Nothing moved. The stillness was total. We were in a world of our own — another world completely cut off from the one we had known. I felt a sense of detachment in this land of nobody — free of disease and interruption.

My mouth fell open.
My heart missed a beat.
Adrenaline swept through my soul.
I could see eternity.

God was an artist, a perfectionist.
This was the final panorama, the closing performance.
I was swept from the cliff
And faded into oblivion.

We were happy as we glissaded back down a steep snowfield, arriving back at our tent late in the afternoon under bright moonlight. Bobby and Runner had gone, taking the sledge and tent with them, leaving a brief note, "Len, gone back to Faraday." I was horrified. They had left me without consideration. It was Saturday; the bar called. This was no place for the animals to perform. I would have to make the journey back to base alone, at night, with no radio or survival equipment. I packed my rucksack, thankful that they had left my sleeping bag. I wished the French luck. They were reluctant to leave me alone, a sin in the Antarctic waste. But I was determined, even stubborn, and rejected their offers of coming with me. They had business to attend to at Petermann. They were planning an expedition across the sea ice far greater than I could attempt, given my obligations to work.

The lonesome moonlit journey across the ice to Faraday was eerie. It was like going somewhere where I had never been before and would never go again. Almost like a wonderful dream. My only means of navigation was to follow Bobby's and Runner's sledge tracks. They had taken our only compass. A light breeze drifted snow across the ice, covering their tracks in places. The journey was risky and the consequences fatal if I became lost or fell into the sea through a covered seal hole or crack in the ice. Fine spindrift snow found its way into my clothes. I feared that a cloud might obliterate the moon — my only means of illumination — leaving me cold and frightened in the dark to die. I made my way slowly through the maze of icebergs that loomed above me. They were giants gazing down on a lone figure that should not be. They looked supernatural in the moonlight. I stopped only to check the direction of the ever-faint sledge tracks. But for all the danger, I was happy. I never felt alone, but I was alone. I often looked back, but there was no one there. I felt on a different plane, a level above what T. S. Elliot captured in his lines in The Waste Land.

Who is the third who walks always beside you?
When I count, there are only you and I together

But when I look ahead up the white road
There is always another one walking beside you
Gliding wrapped in a brown mantle, hooded
— But who is that on the other side of you?

I felt strange, like an outsider looking in, as I approached Faraday. Alice through the looking glass at a world beyond, I did not belong to the world I was about to enter. The generator hummed, breaking the silence of the night. Lights illuminated the complex of snow-covered huts, casting ghostly shadows across the ice. I removed my skis and rucksack and as much of the ice and snow that covered me as possible. I hesitated. I wanted to turn back and return to the ice and snow. I wanted the feeling to remain with me, but it disappeared the minute I opened the door.

It was past midnight. My beard was caked in icicles. Bobby and Runner sat at the bar. Mid-sentence, they stopped putting that bit of the world to right and looked over their shoulders at me in silence.

They just looked at me in disbelief, as if I did not belong
and, perhaps I didn't.

Mid-winter, June 21st, a time to celebrate, a time to love thy neighbour, a time to try and behave as though we all got on with one another. We were almost halfway there, halfway through the endless days until the Bransfield's return — albeit five or six months away! It was all downhill from here on. Supposedly the best half was to come — longer days, the sun high in the sky, fewer storms, travel over the sea ice and, eventually, the return of the animals and the ship. Mid-winter was celebrated by every base in Antarctica, a continental holiday on ice.

Ambrose and Joffs volunteered to publish the mid-winter magazine, a BAS tradition. A revised and censored version would be sent to our families. They, the magazine committee, decided to interview every base member and publish the results.

"What do you like most about being on base, Barry?" asked Joffs.

"Nothing," replied Barry.

"What is your favourite base activity, Barry?"

"Nothing."

"What's the first thing you will do when you leave here?"

"Mind your own fucking business."

"Thank you, Barry. It was very interesting!"

I wondered what Barry's mum would think about that! Did she expect to get the same Barry to return after all he had been through? Would she need to treat an ailing son and help him on the road to recovery when he returned? I wondered how we had changed, how we were different from when we arrived. Would a new arrival be able to see the difference between those of us in our first winter and those in their second? Things would be better after mid-winter, I hoped. Life would get easier. The animals would be tamed, and the quiet ones would come out of their corners.

By tradition, each of us made a gift that was to be raffled before the big meal. For some, making the gift was a chore. Others worked enthusiastically, keeping their handicraft a closely guarded secret. A mid-winter programme of entertainment was planned and, in some cases, rehearsed. Gourmet banquets, amateur dramatics, musical performances, poetry reading and, of course, the struggling magazine were all included in the week-long festival. For a change, there was an air of purpose around the base as we prepared for the big day. For some it was a step closer to going home and a time to plan. For me, it was a step closer to the next winter and repeating the process all over.

We were informed by BAS who was coming south next season. They told us the names of the new FIDlets who would join us at our Antarctic zoo. This led to much speculation as to who would replace Joffs as the next BC. This was a coveted position, normally given to one of the second year people — or at least someone who had previously wintered elsewhere with BAS. Many thought that Runner was favoured for the job, although he was scheduled to spend his second winter at South Georgia. A new arrival, Colin, was another possibility. Colin had wintered at Halley a couple of seasons previously. He had survived being hit by a low-flying BAS Twin Otter that buzzed the base as he photographed the plane from the top of one of the base huts. Miles Mosley, the BC at the time, was standing next to Colin. He was not so lucky — he was decapitated.

The French arrived in time to join in on the celebrations. The weather had deteriorated just before mid-winter, causing some of the sea ice to break up. So they had a difficult journey reaching Faraday through the maze of broken ice and open leads of water. They smelt stronger than ever of seal blubber and body odour. We all gathered in the bar. Penguin Radio, the Falkland Islands radio station, broadcast a mid-winter programme on our behalf, with music and dedications from our families.

"And for Pete Salino at Faraday we have Rod Stewart with Sailing, and the message is: With all our love from mum, dad and Ben the dog!"

We collapsed in laughter as Pete turned crimson and Ben the dog's idea of Pete's favourite record wailed across the airwaves.

One by one we waited our turn for the message
we wanted to hear.
Some wondered why it did not come and why she had not been in contact for so long.

On mid-winter's day Joffs followed the BC tradition of cooking a late breakfast and serving it up in bed, complete with champagne. Around lunchtime we cleaned up the base and sat in the bar drinking Tequila Sunrises. Each lay his wrapped mid-winter handicraft at the foot of the plastic Christmas tree ready for the mid-winter draw. Joffs was master of ceremonies, neatly dressed in a suit. One by one he picked a gift from under the tree and a name from a hat.

"Don, number two!"

There was a loud applause and whistling as Don, dressed in his party one-piece, bright red, combination long-john, vest and

Captain Bligh hat, stepped forward to receive his beautifully framed photograph of the base that had been made by Ian. The gifts ranged from well-made carpentry to paintings, ornaments and framed photographs. The French joined in with seal skin mugs and half coconuts left over from a warmer part of their world trip. The coconuts had been transformed into cartoon men.

Pint and the waiters went into action, and the eating commenced: Cream of Chicken Soup, King Prawn Provocale, Spaghetti Arabiata, followed by Lime Sorbet. Then we broke back to the bar while the tables were re-set, wine stocks replenished and our stomachs given a chance to rest.

Joffs came in with a huge sack of family presents that had been hidden on base all winter. It was an emotional event with personal letters and gifts from families and girl friends. It was a Christmas atmosphere with a difference, unlike any we had experienced before — except those on their second winter.

Back to the dining room and the banquette: Sea Trout Hollandaise, Upland Goose with Orange Sauce, Roast Baron of Beef, Roast Turkey, Shoulder of Beef with Almonds and Roast Leg of Pork. A selection of deserts, cheeses, coffee, liqueurs and a huge round of applause for Pint completed an excellent meal; we were stuffed. Stomachs were bloated to the extent of bursting, leaving no room for the normal excess of alcohol. So it was a subdued, if not emotional, night in the bar. There were no arguments, no tempers and no heated discussions. For the first time in months we were almost, but almost, united. The gifts from home, the combined effort to make it a successful day and the realisation that we had made it this far left me happy in my Antarctic home.

Pete was of Italian descent. Pete "Pasta" Salino we called him. He was a tall, blonde and blue-eyed met-man in his early twenties. We had travelled south together. Pete differed from other base members in being both animal and quiet one. He was astute and intelligent, but a Jekyll and Hyde. The second mid-winter evening's programme was charades, a perfect game for the animals. There was heavy drinking and raucous behaviour. Pete was drinking heavily as usual.

Bobby jumped to the floor and cavorted in some disgusting pantomime, exaggerated by a brain drowned in alcohol. The rest of us failed to guess the word he was trying to act out.

"Cunt," he blurted, looking between his legs at the audience and pointing vociferously at his anus before falling in a heap, much to the amusement of the other animals. The game was short-lived. It degenerated into the regular heated discussions, and the quiet ones retreated to their corners.

Pete had been a cause for concern. They feared for their safety when he was like this. One minute he was a quiet one and the next an aggressive animal. He was schizophrenic, his eyes and mood would change suddenly. Something clicked in his head. It was as if someone had closed a switch. A tussle broke out and Pete hit Don's head against the wall. Ambrose joined in, knocking Joffs to the floor. We had a fight on our hands. There was bedlam in the bar.

"I've had enough of this!" I said. "Big as you fucking are we're going to sort this out!"

I stood up to Pete. He loomed up at me like a Rottweiler. The others backed away. He put his face close to mine.

"Go fuck yourself. What the fuck do you know anyway? If you wanna fight, let's fucking fight."

His eyes were crystallised. He was not the Pete I went skiing and climbing with. He was possessed. I stood my ground and let him rant. The Rottweiler in him strained, but an invisible leash held him back. The others scurried off, but I stood my ground. He was capable of making mincemeat of me, but my instincts told me that he would not attack. Then, suddenly, as quick as it all began, he broke down weeping. The Rottweiler was reduced to a Poodle, and we all knew. We never discussed the episode, and the threats were never repeated.

We were not inclined to work the days after mid-winter. Often we sat around talking about what we would do when we left Faraday, still twenty months away for many of us! Most planned a South American jolly before returning home. Some, but not many, still had girl friends waiting for them. The French were quite clear what they wanted. They each wanted a new aluminium-hulled yacht with retractable keel, and to set off around the world with a lady of their choice.

Post-mid-winter blues, almost non-existent daylight hours and continual storms kept us on base for what seemed an eternity. But the mood was relaxed with almost no daily routine, and people slept late into the morning. Pint's life was made easier by the mountain of food left over from the banquet, although cold buffet every day started to wear thin with some. The return to a routine of work was a natural progression, mainly forced by a desire to occupy time.

This is the place where time and events have brought us.
This is the place we must survive.
This is the place, and they are the future.
There is time in between before we say good-bye.

9

The storms raged for weeks, and the boredom set in. We tried
new ways to pass the days while the blizzards continued to keep
us indoors. I showed Runner, Don, Andy and Bobby how to
play the Oija board; but the session collapsed in laughter. We received messages from Wendy, Waxy and Big Mack. I suspected
that someone was not taking it seriously! A second game some
days later ended when Bobby collapsed drunk over the board
and Runner slopped off in disgust.

These were difficult days. Tempers grew thin as the weather
continued to imprison us. Bobby stormed off to bed one night
when the others booed at his birthday choice of film. Ian jumped
up and down above Jeff's pit room, waking him, ranting and
raving that he had been put on too many gashes. Pint threw a
tantrum when some-
one raided his food
store. He found the
person tucking into a
huge English breakfast

one morning, using up rations that had to be eked out over the winter months ahead. Ambrose served up curried beans one Sunday dinner and spoilt another day. It only took one person to bring down the mood of the whole base.

But eventually, in mid-July, the weather improved. People forgot their grievances, donned their skis and struggled up Woozle through the deep snowdrifts deposited by the storms. The sea ice was still intact despite the battering it had taken. In fact, it was even stronger than before with a huge build up of snow on top of the ice. The days were getting longer. At last it looked as though we could begin our winter travel in earnest. The French left on an ambitious trip to sledge as far south as they could, or dared, crossing unpredictable sea ice. I felt envious of their freedom as I watched them haul their laden sledge south.

Field parties regularly left base headed for various locations within the limits of our permitted travel. The weather was extremely variable, and large cracks and expanses of open water appeared in the sea ice. But the ice that remained was thick and strong. I set off on my second attempt to climb Shackleton, this time with Pete and Andy. We reached the mainland in record time by attaching our sledge to the back of a skidoo driven by Joffs. We held on to long ropes attached to the sledge. We hurtled behind on skis, weaving through a minefield of lumps of ice, and flying over drifts of snow heaped up everywhere. Headlong tumbles into snowdrifts were common, bringing the train to an abrupt halt with shrieks of laughter. Once again I was happy, delighted to be where I was doing what I loved – the outdoors. We hauled all our mountaineering equipment up the Rasmussen ramp and settled in for the night, leaving a base camp with the sledge and our pyramid tent at the foot of the ramp for our return.

Early the next morning we skied up the edge of the Wiggins Glacier, this time carrying everything on our backs. But the heavy rucksacks constantly caused us to break through surface snow into gaping crevasses below. It was a frightening experience with legs dangling in free space, knowing that the rest of your body could follow at any moment. The rope stretched between us was our line between life and falling into a pit and certain death. We camped in failing light below the north face of Mount Peary high on the wrong side of the glacier from Shackleton.

The noise of snow and blocks of ice avalanching from Peary as the morning sun touched its summit woke me sharply. I thought of the three FIDS who lay frozen there. One day their bodies would fall in a block of ice, then flow in the glacier below us and out into the Penola Straight. It was bitterly cold. It summoned all our energy to break camp and be ready to continue our journey.

All day we picked our way across the Wiggins Glacier, searching for ice bridges to cross the sea of crevasses that hindered our passage. We rested when we thought we were safe on solid ice. The danger of a snow bridge collapsing under us increased as the sun warmed the glacier. I felt minuscule and vulnerable. Each step took us further from Faraday. Rescue would have been impossible. There was no room for mistakes. We continued up to where the Leay Glacier branched from the Wiggins, divided by Shackleton as the flow of ice found the easier path past the mountain on its downhill journey. The days were short, and the climbing was hard on our bodies after months of inactivity. It was some time before we found a relatively crevasse-free campsite. We huddled into our sleeping bags before cooking a meal and trying to sleep.

All night the glacier heaved and creaked below us. We half expected a gaping hole to open up in the ice and swallow our camp without a trace. The night temperature dropped to -25°C. Moisture from our breathing froze to the inside of the tent, covering our faces, sleeping bags and equipment in hoarfrost. Ice dropped from the walls as the tent flapped in a gentle breeze blowing up the glacier.

In the morning it took me less than a minute to prime the paraffin stove and dive back into my sleeping bag for warmth, waiting for the heat from the stove to warm the tent while a pan of snow was converted into something drinkable. But it was a minute too long. I lay shivering, listening to the hiss of the stove while ice on our frozen clothes melted and dripped down, wetting our sleeping bags. I sat up to prepare breakfast. I tried to get as much of my body as possible in the higher, warmer part of the tent, almost asphyxiating myself in the oxygen-starved carbon monoxide-rich air. I opened the tent to collect more snow, and it filled with a rush of icy air. I kept the tent sufficiently open to keep a healthy balance of air and warmth. The stove was not extinguished until we had eaten breakfast and dressed for the cold. It was still dark as we silently packed our rucksacks with equipment and left for the summit of Shackleton, leaving our camp intact on the glacier. Six tall red flags surrounded our tent to make its position more visible should the weather deteriorate. Had we lost our campsite, our chances of survival would have been slim.

The only sound to penetrate the darkness was the creaking of our crampons digging into the surface under our weight. The lifeline snaked between us, leaving a thin trail in the fine surface snow. Soon it was covered by spindrift as the breeze turned and started to blow down the glacier bringing colder air from above. I felt good.

We found our way through the field of crevasses to the relatively crevasse-free summit ridge. The morning sun relieved the bitter cold. The views back down the Wiggins Glacier and across to Peary became more spectacular as we gained height. This was a mountaineer's utopia.

Close to the summit our attempt to climb Shackleton was thwarted by a ten-metre wall of ice. We did not have the necessary equipment to climb this wall, but it was of no real consequence. We were in the mountains, and another one hundred metres made no difference to our enjoyment of the climb. From our vantage point high on Shackleton we were able to pick out an easier route back to our camp, avoiding many of the difficult crevasses we crossed earlier in the day.

We decided to make another attempt at the mountain the following morning. We moved our camp high onto the ridge early the next morning using the easier, relatively crevasse-free route. The ice pitch proved more difficult than we had anticipated, abounding in dangers not seen the day before. We attempted to find a way around the ice pitch, but the wall refused to succumb to our efforts. And we were faced with an additional, far worse problem; the weather began to deteriorate. We could not contact Faraday, but Palmer station responded to our calls and confirmed that the barometer was falling rapidly.

Defeated, but by no means disappointed, we moved our camp back down the Wiggins Glacier to the foot of Mount Balch and set up our camp, expecting a storm in the night. However, the storm did not develop. The fine weather continued as we woke the following morning. We climbed a couloir, a chimney of ice leading towards the summit of Mount Balch. We gained a shoulder below the summit ridge. The risk of avalanche was high as we climbed a corrie, a steep hanging glacier below the summit. Both Andy and Pete disappeared into deep crevasses but came to no harm. They climbed back up the lifeline to safety using equipment we hung from our harnesses in preparation for such events. Huge cornices hung from the summit ridge like umbrellas over the valley below. We looked back at our trail in the deep snow below, twisting upwards from our campsite which was just a tiny red speck far below. There was no time for celebrations at the summit; the danger of avalanche was real. We retraced our steps in the failing light for a final night on the glacier.

The fine Chilean wine was nicely chilled by the time we arrived back at our base camp at Rasmussen. We feasted on leg of lamb washed down with the wine. We finished with a drop of good malt whiskey before a sound night's sleep on familiar territory. We had been in the mountains for a week and were physically tired but happy. Mountaineering is a wonderful sport.

It is better to wait than take a chance,
to pause than to pant,
to sing than to shout.

"Fire, fire!" shouted someone down the corridor, awakening me from a deep sleep. It was Saturday night, and I was filled with alcohol. A chill ran through my body. The greatest fear of all on an Antarctic base was fire. Faraday would burn like a haystack if a fire caught hold, leaving us homeless. I half dressed, grabbed more clothes and rushed outside. The near corner of the boat shed was gone; the remnants of one wall of the sauna were clearly visible through the flames that roared into the star-filled sky. Burning material showered down onto the base and its surrounds. The main hut and the generator building were scorched but not burning. It appeared that the fire had started in the sauna and was sweeping rapidly through the dry timbers of the boat shed. It threatened to burn the entire base.

Runner got onto the roof of the generator building with the fire hose while Geoff, the diesel mechanic, started up the fire pump. It spluttered into life, and Runner directed the hose expectantly.

"Water, pump the fucking water!" he screamed as he shielded himself from the heat.

Geoff ran about in a panic as a trickle of water emerged from the hose and died.

Joffs organised a chain gang with the few buckets we could find. We collected water from a nearby hole in the sea ice, but our efforts were futile. The corner of the base began to ignite. There was bedlam. Drunken FIDS were running in all directions. Fire extinguishers appeared but had little effect and were soon used up.

"More fire extinguishers. Where's the fucking fire extinguishers!" shouted someone as a loud explosion came from within the burning boat shed and a missile shot into the air.

"Look out. That's the CO_2 cylinders exploding in the fire," screamed Joffs.

Ironically our entire stock of spare extinguishers was stored in the burning boat shed. Cylinders of carbon dioxide exploded in the heat, ejecting missiles vertically into the air or horizontally through the flames. Some passed dangerously close to where we stood, helplessly looking on.

Pint appeared at the door with refreshments. He had been drinking heavily but wanted to help. A missile embedded itself into the door next to him. He dropped the tray of beer in fright and retreated to the dubious safety of the burning base. He went back to the bar to continue his Saturday night festivities. While the fire raged outside he wrote his resignation to BAS.

The fire was spectacular, illuminating our frozen surroundings. One by one we went for our cameras to record the event. There was little else we could do but watch the boat shed crumble, taking with it the sauna, the fire-fighting equipment and all the fresh meat, cheese and vegetables we possessed. A slight breeze miraculously kept the fire from spreading to the other huts.

By early morning the fire had burnt itself out, and the sound of exploding cylinders had ceased. The boat shed and its contents were reduced to a smouldering heap of ash and twisted metal. The surrounding snow was turned black.

"God, what happened last night?" I thought as I stirred from a troubled, brief sleep. My hangover was complete.

During the next day or two we sifted through the debris and recovered some partly cooked meat — meat with the savour of burnt plastic.

"My passport," cried Don. "My passport and money were hidden in there!"
"The porn. All the porn magazines were in the sauna!" cried Bobby.
"Oh shit! The spare met balloons," sighed Tim.
"The food … "

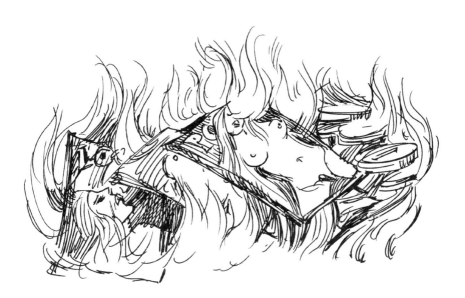

August was a relaxed month on base, helped by good weather. The days were getting longer, beautifully sunny and cold. Everyone who wanted to get away from base for a few days had the opportunity to do so. I often made long ski trips alone around the group of islands in search of wildlife and tell-tale signs of Antarctic spring.

People were now constantly away from base, making the most of the good weather. Spirits were high. Midway through August I once again had the chance for a jolly. This time I set out towards the mainland with Andy and Ambrose.

No sooner had we left base than Ambrose fell through a seal hole, and he had to return to base for a change of clothing. I patiently waited with Andy for Ambrose to return. We passed our time unsuccessfully fishing in the hole through which Ambrose had fallen. Eventually, the three of us hauled our sledge across the sea ice to the mainland. We winched all our mountaineering equipment up the Rasmussen ramp before turning in for the night in a pyramid tent.

The following morning we backpacked to my previous campsite below Mt. Balch. After setting up camp, we completed the day by climbing steep rock and ice to the summit of nearby Mt. Mill.

The next day in brilliant sunshine we repeated our previous route to the summit of Mt. Balch. From our high vantage point we studied at length possible routes up Mt. Peary, the summit of which was only three or four kilometres away. But the summit of Peary appeared different from how it looked from below. There were, in fact, two pinnacles, one higher than the other, crowning the summit plateau. The ill-fated party of FIDS could not have reached the higher summit pinnacle on the day they died, a point called the Tower. More likely they had climbed the lower pinnacle in front of the Tower.

After a good night's sleep we packed our camp and set off across the Wiggins Glacier towards a high pass between Mt. Shackleton and Chaigneau Peak. With overcast skies and poor visibility we were once again surround by yawning chasms and mountains of ice that winded slowly down into the sea, seven or eight kilometres below. By late morning the skies cleared and temperatures plummeted. We gained the pass. We skied down a steep slope into a massive bowl to reach our intended campsite at the foot of Mt. Scott.

Ambrose was showing signs of hypothermia, so we hastily erected the tent, got him into his sleeping bag and lit a stove for warmth. Andy and I left Ambrose and skied across to the south ridge of Mt. Scott to look for a possible route to the summit for the following day. But a jumble of seracs protected the summit, making the route impossible. We returned to our camp as the sun dropped below the frozen horizon and the air temperature plummeted even further. It was bitterly cold under the dazzling starlit sky.

We found Ambrose still shivering in the tent. A careful examination revealed that he had frostbite on his hands, arms and toes. There was no point in showing our anger. He had all too often exposed bare flesh to the cold by not making proper use of his protective equipment. We had constantly reminded him of the dangers, but now he was frost bitten. And we had to get him down out of the mountains as soon as possible.

The next morning was even colder. We left Ambrose in the tent until the last possible moment as we packed for the descent to sea level. Hoarfrost covered our beards and clothing. We worked as quickly as we could to break our camp. None of us had been on the Duseberg ramp before, but it was our nearest ramp. I had passed the ramp many times before at sea level while visiting Petermann and felt sure that we could find a way down out of the mountains. We had to reach Petermann where we could attend to Ambrose.

We started our descent. There was a moment of despair as Ambrose fell and lost a ski; it sped downhill towards a crevasse. The loss of a ski at this point could have proven disastrous. Skis not only provided protection from falling into crevasses but also stopped our feet from sinking into deep powder snow. In Ambrose's case, they also reduced the likelihood of getting more frostbite. Fortunately the ski came to a halt at the very edge of the crevasse. With some difficulty, we managed to recover it and continued our journey down towards the Duseberg ramp.

Eventually we found a route to the head of the ramp and fixed a rope for the descent to sea level. An hour later we were in comparative comfort at Petermann hut with a roaring coal fire. The French were still on their sledge journey south, leaving the Kim alone locked in the sea ice — her bright red hull and deck contrasting sharply with its hostile brilliant white and blue surroundings.

After a good meal and a warm night at Petermann and a long lie in bed the next morning, Ambrose had recovered sufficiently to ski back to our base camp at Rasmussen. We arrived late afternoon. From our base camp, which was fortunately still intact, we radioed Joffs to send a skidoo the following morning to collect Ambrose and our sledge. That would leave us with our mountaineering equipment and emergency supplies. We intended to climb Mt. Demaria before making our way back to base the same evening. We turned in for the night in the comparative comfort of the pyramid tent after a good meal washed down with well-chilled alcohol.

We crawled out of the steaming tent at first light, packed the sledge and set off across Waddington Bay to climb Mt. Demaria. The skies were clear. Ambrose stayed in bed with his thoughts awaiting the arrival of Joffs. Ambrose's ego had been dented by his experience on that journey into the mountains. He was disappointed with his performance. For many on base, the discomfort and high risk of travel in the mountains outweighed the pleasures.

A journey into the desolate wastelands was a euphoric, stimulating experience — one which filled me with joy for weeks and, without which, life on base would have been intolerable.

12

I was working on the roof of the base, trying to repair the met-men's radar, when I spotted the French in the distance hauling their laden sledge towards Faraday. They were returning from their trip south. It was good to see them back on base. They had travelled seventy or eighty kilometres further south to Prospect Point, an old BAS hut on the mainland abandoned in the late fifties. While at Prospect they climbed some of the mountains in the region collecting material for their film and book which were to be published on their return to France.

That evening we dined our guests with a selection of barely edible meat scavenged from the hut fire. It tasted a mixture of plastic, burnt wood, and perhaps even the porn magazines and Don's passport. The meat looked appetising, but it was appalling. I hate to think what effect it had on our health!

The lack of fresh meat inspired Pete to shoot a young Crabeater seal. It was one of the first to appear close to the base at the onset of spring. But the killing of the seal divided the base. It caused deep resentment from some who claimed it was completely unnecessary. To some extent they were correct; we had a large supply of tinned and dried food. Seal and penguin meat was disgustingly repugnant, barely edible — unless you were French! We tried everything to get rid of its awful taste. We hung the carcass for days, we cooked it in curry, we soaked it in wine, we even pickled it. But nothing took away the stench and taste of rotten seafood. Even Pete disliked the taste. He stormed out of the dinning room one night after being goaded into eating it by the people who criticised him for shooting it.

"Why shoot the thing if you ain't gonna eat it? Get it down yer neck, Salino," taunted Runner.

But Pete meant well. None of the alternative choices of meats were popular. On one occasion a cormorant flew into one of the radio aerials and damaged itself beyond repair. It appeared on the dining room table, served in a sweet sauce. Some refused to eat it, but none criticised that we had cooked it, presumably because it would have died anyway. It was the best meat we had eaten in months.

The end of winter was fast approaching. It was a time of indecision. Many of those who were due to remain the following winter were having second thoughts. Pint had already resigned from BAS on the night of the boat-shed fire, deciding that he had had enough of this way of life. His resignation was followed shortly by Bobby's. Bobby decided that he wanted to travel the world and could not wait another one and a half years. Then Andy resigned because he felt the restrictions on travel were too severe. He wanted more freedom to travel further and for longer periods. The spate of resignations meant that only four of us would remain for a second winter on Faraday: Pete, Ambrose, Ian and myself.

By early September spring was well and truly in the air. Penguins waddled and skidded across the sea ice. They arrived from their winter homes as the sun slowly melted back the winter snow, revealing previous year's nesting sites on the islands around Faraday. Brilliant white Snow Petrels hovered high in the sky with their distinctive forked tails. They screamed at us below dare we near their nesting sites on the shear rock faces. Dominican gulls sat patiently on ice flows, watching and waiting for an opportunity for their next meal — even if it was another Dominican's egg or chick. Giant Petrels soared past the base, speeding to some far-off destination to rear their young. Weddell seals cut holes in the ice with their teeth. They gave birth to a solitary pup next to their doorway to the sea. They trusted on the rest of the sea ice remaining intact long enough for the pup to learn how to fend for itself. A hoard of predators would be waiting hungrily below as the ice broke up around them. Crabeater seals gave birth far from land. The births were surrounded by an audience of Dominican gulls waiting to clean up after each new arrival. The Paddies were not able to compete with the larger, more aggressive gulls and soon migrated north to scavenge. The days got longer and the nights less cold as our time for winter travel was rapidly drawing to a close.

I wanted to go on a final jolly before the sea ice completely broke up and we would once again be restricted to the island group. Most of the others were reluctant to travel with me because my trips were ambitious, uncomfortable and exhausting. I teamed up again with Pete and Andy, the strongest pair on base, and we left to sledge south to the limits of our permitted travel area. We travelled over a week, pulling our sledge more than a hundred kilometres over some of the best sea ice Faraday had experienced in years. We had been extremely lucky with the winter conditions. Some years the sea ice failed to form, making it impossible to get off base during the long winter months.

The sledge was difficult to pull over the slushy surface that had been softened by the sun. Embedded into the frozen sea were chunks of glacier ice. We had to climb these and ski down the far side, followed closely by the sledge a ropes-length behind. With luck, the sledge would remain upright and allow us to continue our journey without stopping. But there were surprises. Andy was out in front; Pete and I fanned out on shorter hauling ropes behind. Andy crossed a large lump of ice and skied down to soft snow on the other side. But the water below was not frozen. He sank into the sea, skis and all. We hauled on his sledge line, but it was impossible to get him out of the sea from where we stood on the slippery slope. I cut his hauling line so that he could reach the other side of the open pool of water. I detached myself from my hauling line. Keeping hold of Andy's line, I skied to the other side of the pool and tried to pull him. The thin ice gave way; and I, too, found myself in the water. Struggling for my life, my muscles immediately started to lock in the freezing water. I could barely move my limbs. I desperately tried to haul myself out of the water, but the thin ice constantly broke under my weight. Had Pete also gone into the water, the three of us would have perished, leaving the sledge as our only witness. I found a slab of ice that held as I crawled out. My skin was burning from the cold. Andy made it to safety shortly after. But we were still in danger. Immediately our clothes began to freeze. Pete poured hot coffee that we kept handy on the sledge in anticipation of such an event. We stripped off our frozen clothing and put on spares — dry clothes we kept in the same emergency bag as the coffee. We were very luck to survive.

Our journey took us south following the Grandidier Channel to Lahille Island, then east deep into Beascochea Bay, on north past the Berthelot Islands and, finally, back to Faraday. We camped under impressive, unclimbed peaks and longed for a chance to attempt their summits. We found caves full of Snow Petrels preparing for the busy nesting season. There were tiny islands where penguin colonies went about their daily struggle for centuries. Never did we tire of the scenery, particularly in the Antarctic spring; and it was with reluctance that we returned to our duties at Faraday.

An impromptu Saturday night party at Wordie, to which the French were cordially invited, marked our return to base. Music blared into the frozen night from the old hut. It was brought up to sauna-like temperatures by a roaring coal fire.

"Michelle vill now perform es fire-eating act," announced Bruno. "Everyone outside, now!"

Michelle poured alcohol spirit into his mouth from a can held in one hand while he held a cigarette lighter at the ready in the other.

"Go on, do the dragon!" we laughed, cameras at the ready.

He hesitated while the rest of us looked on expectantly. He blew a fine jet of spirit from his mouth and ignited it with the lighter. A massive ball of fire shot from his mouth into the freezing night air. For one or two brief seconds all was under control, but he had miscalculated the amount of spirit in relation to the amount of puff he had in him. The flame grew bigger as he tried to get rid of all the liquid, almost igniting the old base with the flare of fire. Eventually Michelle ran out of air and was forced to breath in. The ball of fire collapsed and engulfed his head. He coughed out unburned liquid and, taking the fire into his lungs, collapsed to the ground.

"Rothera, Faraday." I made the familiar call to Paul, the Rothera doctor, the next morning as Michelle complained of severe chest pains. Paul waited patiently at Rothera as I struggled with the x-ray equipment, carefully following his instructions. I looked blankly at the negatives for "dark patches" on Michelle's lungs. Whether or not I saw anything significant on the x-rays I will never know, but we diagnosed him as having bronchial pneumonia.

> *And where does all this fit into the pattern of life?*
> *Why are we subjecting ourselves to this?*
> *It's easy;*
> *It's better to say "I've done that," than to wish that you had done it.*

13

A BAS Twin Otter swooped low over Faraday and faded into the background of mountains. It turned for another run, its door open ready to drop our first mail in ten month. Everyone was on the hill to watch the event and photograph something different. The Twin Otter was making its way to Rothera to begin a new field season. It was to fly geologists deep into Antarctica to continue their programme of research. Two large sacks fell from the bright red aircraft landing on target next to the base. A miss could have spelt disaster with the sacks landing in the sea — news from loved ones washed into the Antarctic seas. In one of the sacks were joints of meat, fresh vegetables and Cindy, a blow up rubber doll that some kind admirer presumed we were in need of.

The Twin Otter dipped its wings in salute and continued its journey south. Everyone was evicted from the bar while Joffs and Ian sorted the mail into piles of varying thickness. I stole off

to my room and studied each envelope in turn without opening any of them. I was curious to know who had written and who had not, but I could not bring myself to open them. I wasn't ready for the return to normality or for news of home. Instead I decided to open all the letters from just one person each day.

I went back to the bar without reading anything. Most of the others were silently sitting around reading their letters. Pete sat alone drinking beer.

"You read all yours," I asked him.

"Yeah, all one of them, from the tax man," he laughed.

Bruno came over to join us. He was reading a letter from his brother in France.

"Claude's mudder 'as committed suicide," he said. "An' he don't know it yet!"

Claude was reading a letter from his girl friend, chuckling with delight at whatever she had written. We watched in despair as he opened each letter, laughing and shouting aloud news from home.

"Bruno," he blurted, "oi is yuncle... ." But then the tragic moment came, and Claude went silent. We rushed to console him.

Our lives were changed.
Winter was over.

14

The arrival of the aircraft had marked the beginning of a new Antarctic season and the end of winter. But there was still work to be done, reports to be written, inventories to be checked, outside dumps to be organised and the interiors to be painted. There were letters to be written and lists of personal chores to be completed before embarking on a second winter at Faraday or travelling north as in most cases.

We threw out all the sauna meat and bits of seal. We feasted on a banquet of leg of lamb and pork dropped by the Twin Otter. Michelle was running a high temperature, but stubbornly refused to take any medication until the other French persuaded him to come to his senses. They had to return to Petermann as soon as possible while the sea ice was still intact. But it was not until the end of October, the same day the Bransfield left Southampton, that he was fit to travel. We never saw them again at Faraday before they sailed from Antarctica making the long voyage back to France. The presence of the French close to base, and on base for much of the time, had changed our winter.

The Rothera Twin Otter was forced back to South America to deliver blood samples from two cases of suspected hepatitis. I was going up the hill early one Sunday morning before breakfast to watch for a Twin Otter, but Ambrose called me back to base before the plane arrived. Geoff required urgent medical treatment after he almost managed to weld his eye instead of a piece of metal. He was in a great deal of pain.

After treating Geoff I went up to the bar.

"What the hell happened?" I asked as I looked at Cindy's inflated remains on the floor, covered in tomato ketchup.

"She got pregnant, so we gave her an abortion last night!" Pint said with a smile on his face, still drunk from the night before.

Two days later, with Geoff's eye on the mend, the Twin Otters flew overhead on its return flight to Rothera. It dropped more meat, cigarettes, more steroid injections I was giving one patient for tennis elbow and a rubber repair kit for Cindy! The weather had been overcast and stormy for nearly two months, but it changed for the better as glorious warm sunshine bathed the base for the Otter's return trip. Most of us were dressed in shirtsleeves and shorts as we watched the flypast.

"Base photograph," decided someone.

Trying to organise an activity for the whole base, such as a photograph, was near impossible. But the winter would not be complete without it, and now was the time to take it while the warm sunny weather lasted. Everyone gathered in front of the building facing an array of cameras mounted on tripods precariously balanced in the snow. Fifteen photographers trying to get the same photograph was a shambles, and the occasion soon turned into a snowball fight. A snowball hit a loft window above our heads and knocked it from its frame. The heavy window was badly fitted by some less-than-competent carpenter. It landed on Pete deeply gashing his head. The snow was heavily stained from the fountain of blood that gushed from the wound.

"Rothera, Faraday."

"Easy to do," Paul told me. "He won't feel a thing."

I shaved the back of his head to uncover the wound and injected painkiller into the cut as Paul described. I selected what I thought was the appropriate size of needle and thread and began to stitch. I poked at the mass of subcutaneous tissue. I felt sick. Pete sat patiently as I pushed the curved needle through his skin and stitched best as I could.

"Looks great, Pete, but I'll cover it over for a couple of days to stop any infection," I said looking at my work suspiciously. It looked and was a mess, but I was not going to start again and make us both suffer. I covered the wound so the others wouldn't see it and lose confidence in my surgical ability — if they had any. After a week I removed the stitches, revealing a perfectly healed wound but leaving a five centimetre-long ridge of scarred flesh across the back of his head.

I left base on my final trip of the winter with Tim who had been on base all winter without a break. We went camping on the Jalour Islands for a couple of days to just soak up the sun. We watched a small colony of penguins go about their daily routine. And we collected a few of their eggs for Pint. Penguins lay a second egg if they lose the first. So our appetite for fresh eggs did not have a significant affect on the penguin population.

Others managed to get to Petermann across the decaying ice and helped free Kim from her winter clutches. They helped repair the leak that nearly cost the lives of all the crew. But the long run of brilliant weather had to come to an end sooner or later, and it did in mid-November with a vengeance. Storms lashed the whole of the Antarctic Peninsula, destroying the remaining sea ice at Faraday. Both Twin Otters at Rothera were destroyed in the storm; one lost its wings, and the other its tail plane. This ruined Rothera's summer geological programme even before it began.

After the storms we worked hard at clearing the huge drifts of snow from the walkways around the base. Joffs crushed his thumb with a shovel and was in agony from the pressure of blood below his nail. I used one of Ian's carpenter's drill to perforate the nail, and blood spurted upwards like spray from a whale's blowhole. It covered my face causing me to almost throw up.

"Jesus Christ," I uttered, and squirmed in a distinctly non-professional manner.

Despite the blood and gore I had to admit that I would miss the responsibility in a funny, sadistic sort of way. Most likely we would have a doctor on base next winter, and my newly gained medical expertise would no longer be required.

It seemed as if the Bransfield would never arrive. We counted the days and monitored the ship's progress north as she repeated our journey of the year before. Our mood reached an all-time low as bad weather resurfaced and continued to keep us indoors. I felt particularly depressed, probably for the first time since I had arrived in Antarctica. It was Saturday the 5th of December and we were preparing for our customary Saturday night meal. Pint was drunk. He had been up drinking all the previous night and all that day, finally getting something on the table at ten o'clock that night. We sat in silence as the food was served. Not one of us wanted to be there, but we carried out the actions of the Saturday night tradition to keep the peace. The atmosphere was tense, almost frightening. Andy was in a particularly obnoxious mood. Without warning he pushed his chair back, scooping his plate towards him so that his dinner fell to the floor.

"Oh, fuck," he chuckled unconvincingly, making it obvious that it was no accident.

He scooped the meal back onto his plate with his bare hands and ate the mess with his fingers, stuffing the food into his mouth and spitting fragments onto the table just to make things worse.

"Fuck, this is awful. Let it stop, please let it stop," I thought to myself. I sat there eating in silence, sweat breaking on my forehead. Something had to give. Runner and Bobby Banner became loud and objectionable, teasing and provoking, making snide comments if anyone were foolish enough to speak.

"Off to the toilet, Len," said Bobby, chuckling to himself. He was picking on me to see if I'd dare respond.

"Go fuck yourself you slimy little cunt," I thought. I continued eating without looking up. I had a habit of making an excuse to go to the toilet when the atmosphere in the bar got uncomfortable and then sneaking off to bed. We knew each other's habits more than I liked.

"Fuck 'im, Bobby. He can't take it like a man. Hey Davies, when you gonna fucking resign, cunt. All you wanna do is go home," slurred Runner. "Get the fucking wine Banner you idle cunt."

"Fuck off, get it yerself," said Bobby enjoying himself.

The animals were performing at their best. The silent ones withdrew into their shells, wishing that the ordeal was over. They sat it through so as not to make things worse or face the barrage of insults if they dared leave the table. Barry could take no more. He headed for the kitchen and started washing dishes before the meal was over. When he had done what he considered his share of work, Barry escaped to the solitude of his room. Others followed shortly after.

This was Antarctica at its worst.

15

The Bransfied had a difficult time reaching Faraday. She encountered the worst sea ice recorded in many years and had to break through many miles of solid ice before finally reaching the base in mid-December. Unlike the previous year, some of us skied north to meet the ship. We returned to base with our reward: more mail, a keg of real English beer and the end of winter. There was no jubilation or celebration, just relief that the long winter was over.

The change on base was dramatic. The arguments and bickering stopped, and differences were put to one side if not forgotten. We carried out a lightning relief. Within thirty-six hours the ship was gone again, leaving what seemed an army of people on base. They included replacements for those who would leave Faraday and a whole host of summer visitors.

We worked through Christmas and New Year's eve, stopping only briefly to celebrate. The summer on Faraday was relaxed and enjoyable with few breaks for visitors. The weather was warm, wild and windy, causing extremely high sea swells.

The Bransfield returned to Faraday in March for her final visit. She struggled in the deteriorating weather and came close to running aground when she became trapped between rocks and a large iceberg. When she nudged the iceberg to get free, it collapsed onto the ship, sending lethal chunks of ice splintered across her decks.

The bad weather made it urgent for the Bransfield to leave Faraday, so we worked through the night to unload the remaining base cargo. There was a possibility that the ship could make another visit to Faraday on her return from Rothera, but that could not be guaranteed.

"If you're not staying at Faraday for the winter, board the ship now," came the announcement over the ship's loud speakers. Ambrose, Ian and Pete must have had last minute doubts, as I did. Could I face another winter, a repeat performance of the year before? The colossal highs followed by extreme lows took me beyond the abyss. The temptation to board the ship and leave Faraday was real but brief. A shiver went through my body as the others boarded the launch and were gone.

There was hardly time for parting words as we waved farewell to the Antarctic protagonists, dissidents and philosopher in his red combination, bright red, long-john and vest. For better or for worse, they had been my companions all winter. And now they looked back at Faraday from the Bransfield's poop deck as she raised her anchor.

We heard the sound of the ship's horn fade as she cautiously manoeuvred through the tangle of ice and passed out of sight.

However, before the ship sailed,
I was sworn in as BC for the coming winter.

FARADAY BC

16

The thirteen of us sat in the bar for our first meeting. Joffs was gone, and I led the proceedings. The balance had changed; the quiet ones outnumbered the animals. I could already sense that this winter would be different.

The meeting was rudely interrupted.

"There's a ship anchored off shore," someone commented, interrupting important issues such as gash rota and other routine duties. I went outside to see a tiny wooden-hulled vessel anchored close to the base. They had not announced their arrival, so Ambrose called them up on the radio to find out who they were.

"First Mate Willy here from the RV Hero at your service, Sir," came the reply in a broad American accent. "

The RV Hero was the American Palmer Station supply ship. She must have been all of forty years old and typical of vessels of that day. She was a floating legend.

"Just a social call," said Willy. "Captain Lennie invites some of you nice folks to come aboard for dinner. And some of us would sure like to be invited ashore to visit you guys, if that wouldn't be too much trouble."

Willy spoke in an assertive voice, in orders more than questions.

I knew from previous experience that several days of work were about to be lost. It was obvious that great amounts of alcohol were going to be consumed. That evening, a Gemini crammed full with high-spirited American sailors came ashore in a very heavy sea. Willy was at the helm. He was a Danish-looking, tall blond. He was built like a bull terrier. He had a thick set, square face. It was the sort of face one associated with film stars, rather than a sailor in Antarctica.

"Willy by name and Willy by nature, ha ha ha. Get your little bums in the Gemini if yer goin' to the Hero. Let's go and see the captain. Oh, here's some mail for the Bransfield to post when she next calls. You commin' with us, petal?" he asked, speaking to Ian in a highly suspicious manner.

Willy left the American crew at Faraday while Ian and I accompanied him back to the Hero. All the other FIDS chose to stay on base with the Americans. The massive swells made it difficult to board the Hero from the Gemini. The transfer had to be timed just right to avoid being tipped into the sea. It was an extremely dangerous operation. At one moment the Gemini was almost level with the Hero's deck. The next the inflatable plummeted back down to well below the ship's water line. Willy shouted, "Jump," and we landed sprawled across the teak decks of the legendary little ship. The vessel reminded me of those I had read about in early Antarctic exploration. Shackleton could have as easily been there to meet me. She was nostalgic, Antarctica through and through. Captain Lennie fitted the part. He was a small but powerful, dominant man, with years of Antarctic experience to his credit. He carried personnel and cargo between Punta Arenas in southern Chile and Palmer station. A New Yorker by birth and ex policeman, he entertained me with fascinating stories about his experiences in Antarctica. The ship was dry, but he had an "emergency" supply of alcohol for visitors — although he was tea-total. He talked a lot about his family, his travels and his pet Minke whale. The whale, apparently, always came alongside the Hero when it sailed around the top of the Antarctic Peninsula. He told me how it would raise itself up out of the water as high as it could to get a better look at the ship, and backed up his story with photographs of the amazing creature. We talked late into the night until Lennie reminded me that he wanted to get an early start in the morning. I went in search of Willy to take us ashore, but I could find neither Willy nor Ian.

"Look in Willy's cabin," said one of the crew, pointing to a door.

I opened the door and peered inside. At first I thought I was dreaming. Willy and Ian were locked in a compromising position, not in the least perturbed by my intrusion. They had been drinking whiskey smuggled on board from Faraday. Willy smiled knowingly at me. He gave me the creeps, but I never suspected the gent was bent. Ian was drunk, extremely drunk. The empty whisky bottle lay on the floor.

"Let's go, Ian. Time to get ashore," I said politely and closed the door.

The crew laughed and nudged each other knowingly. They knew their first mate.

Ian and Willy finally emerged. Ian could barely walk. He hung on to Willy as we struggled to get him into the Gemini. The swell had not diminished, and the transfer was equally hazardous. The Gemini crashed into the side of the ship as the swell heaved it up to deck level.

"Jump," shouted Willy, the incident in the cabin behind him.

Ian and I crashed back into the Gemini. With Willy at the helm and Ian at his feet in a drunken stupor we headed for the shore. I could just make out the lights of the base through the spray off the top of the waves in the darkness.

"You had your chance," said Ian, hardly able to raise his head. But Willy seemed to have lost interest.

I moved away until we reached the beach. Willy stayed with the Gemini while I helped Ian up the slipway into the base.

There were more shocks in store for me that night. I entered the bar and found the FIDS cowered in one corner. One of the American seamen wielded a knife in one hand and a near-empty bottle of whiskey in the other.

"Come on you limey cunts! Which of you is a man. I'll take the whole fucking lot of yees,"' he shouted, jabbing the knife threateningly at the cowering FIDS.

The FIDS moved back even further. It was like a bad dream.

"The whole fucking world has gone crazy," I thought.

"Come on, you lot, get yer fucking asses down here. The captain's waiting," came Willy's voice over the radio.

"Fucking bastard," shouted the knife-wielding drunken sailor at the radio. He slammed down the radio and smashed it on the floor.

"Fucking bastard," he repeated, as he stamped on the radio. Willy was silenced.

I moved towards the drunken sailor. I felt that somehow I had to get them off the base. The other Americans in the bar seemed oblivious to the dilemma. They were intent on finishing off the whiskey after weeks on a dry ship. Somehow I persuaded him to put the knife away. I ushered them towards the door, encouraged by bottles of whiskey, like donkeys with a carrot. They staggered down the slip towards the waiting Gemini, smashing most of the whiskey on the hard concrete as they went. Willy appeared out of the darkness and moved towards the waiting Gemini.

"Why the fuck don't you answer the radio?" he shouted, obviously annoyed.

I wondered if the smashed radio was still in the bar, but I wasn't going back to look for it and risk having the Americans follow for more whiskey. Not without a struggle and endless good-byes, we managed to get everyone into the flimsy boat and pushed out to sea, relieved that they had finally gone.

The overcrowded Gemini bobbed about in the swell as they tried to get the outboard started. The wind had increased and there was now the danger of brash ice to contend with.

"Fucking queer," one of them screamed as a fight broke out in the Gemini. There was a tangle of arms and legs as they fought each other in a drunken brawl. The boat lurched and there was a sudden upward heave. Willy left the Gemini vertically as if defying gravity, mastering the ability to fly.

"Take yer faggots disease with you, fuckin bender," came a cry, as gravity took over and Willy landed in the frozen sea.

"Oh fuck, he's going to die," I thought. My mind raced to how quickly we could get the dinghies launched. I imagined Willy losing consciousness in the frozen sea. Somehow reversing their intention to murder Willy, the sailors got him back into the Gemini and disappeared into the night towards the Hero and a far-from-happy Captain Lennie.

> *What shall we do with the drunken sailor?*
> *What shall we do with the drunken sailor?*
> *What shall we do with the drunken sail ... or*
> *early in the morning?*

raday. Lemaire Channel in background between Booth Island and Mount
ott.

DS at Faraday

Port Stanley, Falkland Islands

Gypsy Cove, Falkland Islands

RS Bransfield, South Shetlands

Captain and Sue Lawrence

Shackleton's Memorial Cross, Grytviken

King Edward Cove and Grytviken, South Georgia

Abandoned whaling vessels, Grytviken

RS Bransfield breaking ice

Wordie Hut, Faraday

Leopard seal

HMS Endurance

World Discoverer, Faraday

ggins Glacier and Chaigneau Peak

unt Shackleton

Crevasse

Pete (left) and Andy crossing sea ice to mainland

Base camp on sea ice and ramp to glacier above

eopard seal and wind surfer

ur seal and telephone box

Kevin, John and Ambrose leaving for Petermann

John (left) and Kevin at mid-winter

Ice cave, Faraday

Ambrose in radio room

Memorial cross, Petermann

Young Weddell seal

King penguins

Adelie penguins

...lley above the ice

DS at Halley

Dale the builder

Emperor penguins

Hellicopter, Halley

Ex-hellicopter, Halley

rora over Halley

idoo, Halley

Memorial cross, Rothera

Sno-Cat, Halley

Extending Armco garage entrance, Halley

Mid-winter, Faraday

Rothera

Kim anchored at Petermann

Graham, Faraday

17

Steve Martin was a well-spoken, astute person. We had travelled south together on the Bransfield. He impressed the other FIDS as being a knowledgeable, responsible person. It seemed odd that he had taken a job with BAS as a base assistant. By his manner one would have expected him to be an academic. But he had given up studying medicine for personal reasons and accepted a job with BAS, vowing one day to return to his beloved studies.

During my journey south we landed at the BAS research station on South Georgia to drop off Steve and other FIDlets before going on to Faraday. The island had a special place in my heart. It was the gateway to Antarctica and featured heavily in the history of early Antarctic exploration. I was a prolific reader of it. James Cook was the first to land on the island. He arrived there little more than two hundred years before me. He named the island after King George III. I felt honoured at having the opportunity to visit the island.

The base was steeped in nostalgia. The spacious, homely building was maintained well. The walls were lined with wood, glistening with varnish. They were decorated with souvenirs from the whaling era and gifts from visiting ships and private mountaineering expeditions. South Georgia's highest peak, Mount Paget was 1,000 metres of tangled ice and rock, strikingly resembling Mont Blanc.

The abandoned whaling station at Grytviken was just a few minutes walk around King Edward Cove from the base. The beach at the cove was littered with massive whale vertebra and rib bones. The whaling plan, up which the carcasses were once dragged, was intact. Two Argentine whaling ships, derelict and plundered, lay at the broken wooden jetty. It was easy to imagine a big Blue, thirty metres long and weighing a hundred and seventy thousand kilograms, being hauled up the ramp by the massive, rusted winches. I imagined waves of blubber shuddering through the whale's corpse as it made its slow, final journey. I imagined its mouth gaping as the blubber flattened across the plan under its immense weight. I imagined the cutters inserting their long-handled, curved knives to divide their plunder. I visualized fat gulls screeching overhead, fighting amongst the mixture of blood, guts and unwanted bones being flushing back to sea where the next whale lay ready to be hauled up the ramp. As I walked through the abandoned whaling station, my head filled with the murderous stench of the industry.

The old oil vat was still intact and full of the precious oil used to scent the bodies of people who were either ignorant of or indifferent to the destruction caused by this industry. Workshops were still stocked with tools, spares and materials used to keep the little whaling boats at sea. Light penetrated the blacksmith's workshop through a sheet of metal missing from the roof. Decaying bellows lay silent against the coal forge, and the smithy's hammers hung above his dusty anvil. Racks of rusting steel lined one wall. Papers lay scattered on the floors of the offices. Some foreign sailor, who still hunted whales, must have pillaged the old base for souvenirs and saw no value in the carefully hand-written records. The kitchens were bare, except for a broken coal stove and wooden storage cabinets painted bright green. The kitchen tools were probably being used to decorate a bar or the country home of one of the souvenir hunters. Despite the looting, the character of the station was intact. And walking among the collection of partly destroyed wooden huts, I felt the whaler's ghosts live on.

Whaling was a seasonal occupation lasting just four months. Then the fattened whales migrated northwards to their breeding grounds in tropical waters. A skeleton staff was left to maintain the station and prepare for the following season. When whaling was halted due to depleting stocks, the whalers never returned, leaving the whaling station derelict but intact. As distasteful an industry it was, the many abandoned whaling stations around South Georgia made a fascinating museum to that period of history.

The whalers left another legacy to South Georgia — wildlife. Some species were left intentionally and others unintentionally. Some still remained. They introduced two herds of deer that were isolated from each other by a glacier. The herds had survived on South Georgia. BAS had culled the herds to maintain a population sustainable in the harsh environment with scarce food.

The whalers had left behind domestic cats. The cats that remained were emaciated and led a miserable existence in a climate totally unsuitable for them. They fed mainly on bird's eggs, carcasses and afterbirth during the summer. They were herbivorous in winter. Their thin coats offered little protection from the cold and driving snow. It kept their population low.

By far the worst of the sailors' legacy was the rats that infested every part of coastal South Georgia. They had a serious impact on the ecology of the island. Many schemes were considered to exterminate the vermin. But each plan would have affected other wildlife on the island, so none was ever carried out.

The rats could be found even high up some glaciers in huts used by the BAS scientists.

The Norwegian cemetery was located on a convenient strip of land overlooking the whaling station. One cross dominated the tiny burial site, the Boss' last resting place. He was my hero, the reason for me being in Antarctica. Accounts of his adventures left a lasting impression on me. I had been determined to stand where Ernest Shackleton had once stood in Antarctica. He had moored his ship, the Quest, for the last time at Grytviken on the 4th of January, 1922. He suffered a massive heart attack in Rio weeks before, but he insisted on continuing his third Antarctic expedition in his quest of fame and fortune. He planned to circumnavigate Antarctica, to map uncharted coasts and search for valuable mineral deposits.

Shackleton was excited at returning to South Georgia. Years earlier he had gained fame, but not fortune, in a fifteen-month expedition. It ended on South Georgia after his ship, the Endurance, was crushed by ice at 59ES. This expedition was to be the first crossing of Antarctica. Concurrently, his fellow countrymen were fighting the Germans in World War I. He lost his ship. And he very nearly lost his life and the lives of his crew in the Expedition. It became one of the classic adventures in the history of Antarctica.

His surgeon, Dr. Macklin, was called to his bedside early on the morning of the 5th for the last time. "You're always wanting me to give up something, what is it I ought to give up?" Shackleton asked Macklin.

"Chiefly alcohol, Boss. I don't think it agrees with you."

Minutes later Shackleton died. He was buried alongside the Norwegian whalers with whom he felt at home.

Shackleton was reported to be a deeply superstitious man. He went to visit a fortune-teller just before he sailed from England in the Quest. She told him that he would die at 48. Had he lived another 41 days, the fortune-teller would have been right!

During my visit to South Georgia, the lure of Antarctica had taken hold of me. And I was eager to get to Faraday. I recalled what Shackleton had said when he received the news that Scott had died attempting to be the first man to reach the South Pole.

He did not mean to die in Europe.
He wanted (some day) to die away on one of his expeditions
and, said Shackleton, "I shall go on going, old man, 'till one day I
shall not come back."

18

Steve Martin was appointed BC of South Georgia in his second year. That meant, like me, he was also sworn in as a magistrate to the British Antarctic Territory. Being a magistrate on a BAS base was normally only a nominal title. There was usually little demand for the registration of births, marriages or deaths on Antarctic bases. However, as magistrates we were required to report to Rex Hunt, the governor of the Falkland Islands, any incident that we considered to conflict with British interests in Antarctica. However, the whole of South Georgia was under the strict control of the Falkland Island governor, and it was Steve's responsibility to help administer this control.

The BAS bases kept in constant communication with each other, using the same radio frequencies. The Bransfield was heading north but was still in the vicinity of the Falkland Islands. I overheard Steve request a radio communication with Rex Hunt, an unusual request simply because nothing ever happened on base which would have been of particular interest to him. I sat by the radio and, when Rex Hunt eventually spoke with Steve, I listened in to the conversation with interest.

"A party of people has landed at Leith, and they appear to be collecting metal on the jetty ready to load onto a ship," reported Steve. "They're flying the Argentine flag from the station."

Steve described to Rex Hunt in great detail what he had seen from a vantage point overlooking the old whaling station at Leith. Rex Hunt instructed Steve to go to Leith and take a message to the captain of the ship, the Bahia Buen Suceso. It was moored at the jetty. The message instructed him to remove the Argentine flag from the whaling station. The message also instructed the Argentines that neither military personnel nor firearms were allowed ashore on the island.

Rex Hunt and his wife, Mabel, with Lord and Lady Buxton, a film crew, and a Royal Navy photographer had visited Faraday the previous summer. They arrived on the HMS Endurance. It had been a brief but eventful visit.

"Now remember, if you want your mums to see you on television, don't look at the camera."

"Take 1," called the film crew producer.

Bobby had been in his element. "Hi mum," he grinned, waving at the camera.

"Banner, fer fuck's sake shut the fuck up and listen to the geezer!" shouted Runner.

It wasn't an easy day for the film crew. I sat on a stool next to an announcer whose face I knew, but whose name escaped me. He was a quite man with little interest in getting to know any of the FIDS. Instead, he kept his eyes closed and recited what he was going to say when they shot the take. I listened intently as the announcer spoke to the camera for his introductory opening lines. He was extremely knowledgeable on Antarctic affairs. Without warning he pointed the microphone at me. "And what do you miss most about being here in Antarctica?" he asked.

I froze and just looked at him blankly, then gazed around the room. What the hell did he expect me to say — trees, sex, my dog, oh, and then there was the lost opportunity on the World Discoverer the previous day with Judith. I hoped he would take the microphone away, but the long embarrassing pause seemed to go on for eternity.

"Cut," and everyone relaxed while the announcer re-thought his tactics.

He repeated his opening comments with uncanny accuracy, but this time turned to Bobby. The verbose Scott from Pitlochry was finally a film star.

Bobby and Runner were now on South Georgia with Steve. They had agreed to stay there for a few weeks during the summer to help refurbish parts of the old base. I thought about the previous summer, the animals and the quiet ones, Don and his technicolour one-piece outfit. The film crew had gone about its business. I gazed out the window as the film session progressed; I lost interest in it. The Endurance's photographer was taking photographs of an able seaman, who I later discovered had the most unlikely name of Scott! He posed for photographs while seated on a stationary skidoo on the ice. The skidoo engine was started so that the photographer could get motion shots of Able Seaman Scott of the Antarctic. I saw someone pointing to the controls and another explaining how to drive it. Then they stood back for the photographer to get his material. Suddenly, the skidoo lurched forward at full throttle and sped away at breath-taking speed with Scott frozen at the controls, his mouth wide open either screaming or trying to scream. The skidoo launched itself over an ice cliff plunging into the freezing sea below, taking Able Seaman Scott of the Antarctic with it. I ran out of the bar and down the stairs. I grabbed a rescue bag on the way with all the necessary equipment to rescue Able Seaman Scott of the Antarctic, pursued by the crew.

Able Seaman Scott was very fat, obese in fact. He wallowed in the sea like a bloated whale fighting for his life. Twenty FIDS hauled on a long rope and pulled the numb, blue-faced seaman back up the cliff. He slithered across the ice like a drowned rat. The cameramen were delighted with their unique footage. We tossed Scott into a scalding shower to help revive him. Able Seaman Scott of the Antarctic's television rating was far higher than mine!

The Pebble Mill film team wandered around the base looking for more footage, and I returned to the bar to help entertain our distinguished guests

"Another gin, Mabel?" I asked Rex's wife.

"I'll get that!" said Rex before Mabel could reply. He poured her a few drops of gin into a full glass of tonic. I sat at a table chatting with Mabel. Rex and the Buxtons left for a tour of the base. She pushed her glass towards me, and I filled it with pure gin.

"Where were you before your husband became Governor of the Falkland Islands?" I asked politely, wondering if she, too, was a philosopher. I was sure that she had passed the dividing line after consuming more than four Gin and Tonics.

Mabel nodded a little incoherently while sipping at the gin. She sat facing me with her back to the door, trying to formulate an answer to my question. Don came into the room wearing his one-piece, bright red, combination long johns and vest. He had found his Captain Bligh hat, which had long been lost somewhere around the base. I watched in amazement as he removed every bit of clothing, except for the hat, and stood stark naked behind Mabel as she asked me to repeat the question.

"What's the name of the ship in Mutiny on the Bounty?" I asked her, tears running down my cheeks.

"Bollocks," whispered Don in a voice only Mabel could not have heard as Don tried to swing his testicles above her head.

"B.o.u.n.t.y," she laughed. "You can't catch me on that one!" she said as Don shook his head and jerked his testicles even higher in an act of defiance.

"Bollocks. Where the fuck is Rex?" I thought as Mabel downed the rest of her gin.

Truly, Don was a philosopher and the answer to his question was now clear — to Don everything was bollocks. He was a master of debate. It only needed Mabel to turn round or for Rex and the Buxtons to return, and the most interesting philosophical discussion that I was ever likely to hear would have taken place. Unfortunately, neither happened, and the discussion never took place. But for Don it was a meaningful experience, all part of being a FID. He replaced his clothing and set off in search of a sympathetic ear.

Steve Martin had delivered his message to the Argentines as Rex Hunt had requested. On the 21st of March he set up an observation post to spy on the suspicious activities taking place at Leith.

"There's about a hundred of them, and they have taken over the old BAS base," he reported. "They appear to be making themselves at home and have even shot some reindeer. I told them that they had to report to the BAS base at Grytviken before they landed at Leith or anywhere else on South Georgia."

Steve had visited Captain Briatore of the Argentine vessel Bahia Buen Suceso. It appeared that their purpose was to remove the scrap metal from the old whaling station. There was a great deal of it.

"Many thanks for the information, Steve," replied the Governor. "I want you to continue monitoring what they are doing. Report to me immediately if there are any new developments."

The Argentine scrap metal merchants must have just missed the French yacht Isasis. During the previous winter we received news that they had reached South Georgia and had anchored at Leith. Claudine had given birth to her baby, whom she named

Leith. The baby was the first to be registered born at the whaling station. She was registered in Stanley as Leith 1.

When I visited South Georgia, I had been able to walk over the hill to Leith. I recalled the huge valuable phosphor bronze propellers I saw laying scattered along the beach close to the jetty. Half-buried in sand, the propellers were still gleaming despite having been abandoned and washed by the sea for more than fifty years. The scene was very similar to that at Grytviken. Blacksmith's tools were racked in there by the hundreds. The forge had been left ready to be re-lit. Sheets of iron, some two centimetres thick, lay ready to repair damaged whaling vessels. I had wondered why some entrepreneur never recovered so much metal, it was possibly worth a seven-figure sum. The answer probably included the facts that the abandoned whaling stations were the property of the Falkland Island Territories and that the cost of a ship to recover the metal might not justify the value. But now it appeared that the Argentines were going to take it anyway.

Rex Hunt obviously considered the Argentine presence a threat. At Faraday, the summer season was just days behind me, and I had barely started my second winter on base. There was a great deal of work to do before the onset of winter. The events on South Georgia were in the "outside world," events remote from our Antarctic home. But still, the events were close to a BAS base. We monitored them with the great interest as they began to quickly escalate.

The Endurance was sent to Grytviken with twenty-two marines on board. The Bahia Buen Suceso had long since left. It had left a number of people at Leith. And another Argentine vessel, the Bahia Paraiso, arrived with military personnel and machinery. We listened to Steve's reports, bewildered and with growing concern.

"We are receiving reports of Argentine warships heading towards the Falkland Islands... ."

The BBC World Service announcer described events in Buenos Aires and the build up of military activity in Argentina. I thought back to a conversation with Captain Barker the previous summer. The Endurance Captain told me, "The Argentines will try to take the Falkland Islands by force in the near future. I've warned the Government, but they won't listen. Now they want to scrap the Endurance, the only military vessel we have operating in and around the Falklands!"

He was bitter listening to the broadcast on the BBC World Service and the concern expressed over current military activity in Argentina.

"Mark my words. I will be the last Governor of the Falkland Islands," predicted Rex Hunt during the same conversation.

We knew that the Bransfield was somewhere close to the Falkland Islands. The Biscoe had been in Montevideo undergoing repairs. But we could not have imagined at the time that that the Biscoe was ferrying British marines to the Falkland Islands. The Endurance was occupied elsewhere, somewhere between the Falkland Islands and South Georgia. It had left a number of marines on base with Steve. We listened to the World Service in disbelief as the Argentine ships continued their advance on the Falkland Islands — the build up of what appeared to be war.

Rex Hunt broadcast live to the island population on Penguin Radio. We listened to what he had to say. Coincidentally, it was April Fools' Day, and the time for practical jokes. He advised the Falkland Islanders that the Argentines were expected to arrive the following morning. We could only guess what preparations the few marines at Moody Brook were making and what Captain Barker would be doing with the limited fighting capabilities of the Endurance.

"Is this real?" I asked myself, over and over again. But it was real and escalating.

"Stay in your homes. Do not resist. If Argentine soldiers approach you, do as you are asked." The disc jockey was in a sombre mood. "We will relay the Governor's messages as long as we can," he said, and his next piece of music filled the airwaves.

There was a sense of despair in the Governor's voice. He kept up the dialogue every hour as he received it from his military commander, Major Norman. The major had only assumed command that day. I imagined the Kelpers in their homesteads, dispersed throughout the islands, listening to the same broadcast, fearing for their future.

"What will we do if they come here?" Ambrose asked. Each of us had the same question.

My thoughts turned to the three .303-calibre rifles I kept in the BC's office and the three hundred rounds of ammunition locked away in the safe.

Most of us stayed up all night listening to Rex Hunt's broadcasts. They became continuous with the first sighting of an Argentine warship in the early hours of the morning.

"Argentine ships have been spotted at Mengary Point," reported Rex. "And the sound of helicopters were heard near Port Harriet."

I wondered where Mabel was at the time while Rex kept up the dialogue from his home radio, calming the population as much as he could. An invasion by Argentina, a country that never relented on its claim to sovereignty over the Falkland Islands, was the islanders' greatest fear. The Argentines' claim to sovereignty was steeped in complicated history. It was intensified by the expectation of finding mineral resources in the region. The Argentine government was an ailing military government, desperate to hold on to public support. They were using the reinstatement of the Falkland Islands to Argentina as a means to remain in government.

"Argentine forces are reported to have landed at Mullet Creek," Rex went on. "The marines are stationed at strategic points and are instructed to resist any landing by the Argentines."

His voice was nervous. Few governors to the United Kingdom had ever gone through the nightmare of having his jurisdiction invaded by an aggressive foreign force. Rex Hunt must have known that he was the Argentine's target as head of the Falkland Island administration.

"We are receiving reports of heavy gunfire at Moody Brook, and Argentine soldiers are making their way into the town. I repeat, stay indoors. Do not resist. May God be with us."

We sat in the bar listening to the radio patched through by Ambrose from his radio room. It was six in the morning, and a war was raging. The reception was weak, and the Governor's voice was occasionally lost as the signal faded into the static on the radio. The episode unravelling before us was unreal. The sound of gunfire came over the radio.

"There are Argentines soldiers in front of my house," he stammered. I could sense his fear.

"I'm speaking from under the kitchen table, and they are firing at the house."

We heard more shots and loud bangs.

"I don't know for how much longer I can go on transmitting," he screamed, justifiably afraid.

"May God be with us all," he repeated, and the radio went dead.

I thought he had been killed.

I slept briefly before tuning into the World Service. "Argentine forces invaded the Falkland Islands last night. There are no reports of injuries among the British population, but reliable sources on the islands inform us that a number of Argentines were killed during the battle. Governor Rex Hunt has been removed from office. He was driven out of Stanley wearing full ceremonial dress, including plumed hat and sword. He is on his way to Montevideo in Uruguay."

The World News reported that the fighting lasted for three hours until dawn. The sky-blue and white Argentine flag was flying at Government House. The Argentine Junta declared the islands and their population to be Argentine. Five Argentine soldiers were reported dead, and many others had been wounded.

The World Service broadcast the voice of Margaret Thatcher and angry sentiments in the House of Commons. Cable and Wireless, not surprisingly, failed to come up for their routine telex transmissions. We had lost our main lifeline with the outside world. The Bransfield left the area and continued her journey back to the UK. There was little they could do for us in Antarctica.

It was early morning, and I was numbed by the events of the previous night on the Falkland Islands.

"Fawaday, Fawaday, this is Wed Plum, over."

I could hardly make out the voice on the radio, but the caller repeated.

"Fawaday, Fawaday, this is Wed Plum, over."

"Ambrose, who the fuck is Red Plum?" I asked.

"Dunno," he said.

"I know that voice; it's fucking Barker on the big red ship Endurance! Red Plum! Silly cunt!"

"Red Plum, Faraday," replied Ambrose with a wide grin across his face.

"Fawaday, Wed Plum. I cannot divulge our real name or the position of our ship. But we will provide Faraday with all necessary assistance. If you require assistance, call us on this frequency, over."

Ambrose nearly blew the British defence by calling Red Plum by her proper name. "Endur … err … um, Red Plum, your offer of help is much appreciated. Many thanks."

HMS Endurance signed off, and we were left to wonder …
A Governor under his kitchen table …
A Red Plum in Antarctica …
We were at war …

19

There is a cardboard cut-out, picture book charm about Port Stanley with its brightly coloured wooden houses clustered close to the sea. The most southerly cathedral in the world dominates the small town, really a city. It is the only city as such on the Falkland Islands. The surrounding hills and countryside reminded me of Unst on the Shetland Islands. The tightly knit houses were typical of Patagonia.

Port Stanley has a special attractiveness. The quaint wooden houses, tidy narrow streets and unique well-stocked shops do not exactly give the town a British appearance. But it had characteristics similar to some of the more remote parts of the British Isles. I recalled how Rex Hunt had driven past in his unmistakable, red, London taxi. I recalled the Logger Ducks that waddled around the shore in front of the town in search of food. I recalled the Kelpers, the islanders known for farming the iodine-rich seaweed that blanketed the shores around the islands, how they kept their heads down as they passed and ignored us visitors.

The islanders had Penguin Radio, Penguin News and the BBC World Service to keep them up-to-date with all the news. Television was something for the future. Amateur radio was popular, if not essential. It was a means for communicating between remote farmlands scattered across the islands that covered an area as big as Wales. Stamps were the main island industries. But sheep farming and tourism were a close second and third. I saw an amazing, colourful array of first-day covers that had been issued over the years.

When I had first gone ashore on the Falkland Islands, nobody needed to ask who I was. Dressed in my BAS-issued, bright red anorak, everyone knew that I was a FID bound for Antarctica. I liked the Falkland Islands. I felt at home. They brought back memories of the years I had lived in the Scottish islands. I had given up a teaching career. And the idea of teaching in the Falkland Islands after my work in the Antarctic appealed to me. I imagined myself as a peripatetic teacher of mathematics, travelling freely around the islands — but leaving free time to explore every nook and cranny of the coastline. There was no secondary education in the Falkland Islands. Most children went on to study at the British School in Montevideo. I called in to see John Fowler, the director of education. He was extremely responsive to my idea. He took me around the school in Stanley and, with good reason, proudly showed me the work he and his staff were doing.

"That's Mount William," said John, pointing to a hill three or four miles away as we walked around the school grounds.

Hills and mountains attracted me like a magnet. I left John to his work and followed the main road out of town heading towards Mount William. I passed Moody Brook, the Royal Marines barracks, which housed a handful of marines supported by the Endurance. I made my way over boggy fields and easily climbed to the summit. I sheltered among damp rocks from a cold westerly wind that blew in hard from the moorland that stretched to the horizon.

Somewhere concealed among the low hills below lay the settlements of the eight hundred sheep farmers and their families. Three hundred kilometres further on was Argentina. I looked down towards Port Stanley and its surrounding, heavily indented coastline. The Bransfield's bright red hull contrasted sharply with the bleak surroundings.

The weather and the surrounding scenery reminded me of home and the Yorkshire Moors where I spent so many of my weekends walking or climbing the granite rocks. I started to feel melancholic until a pair of Turkey Buzzards circling overhead, anxious for me to leave their nesting area, brought me back to earth and think of the adventure which lay before me in Antarctica.

I visited one of the three pubs in Stanley. It was like a time gone by — as if the clock had stopped twenty years ago. Kelpers were propped up a bar. They filled the room with smoke and spoke to each other in Kelper's speak, keeping their voices low even though they knew what they were saying was beyond my comprehension. Not even the barman acknowledged my presence, and I felt conspicuously out of place. I drank my beer in less time than it took to order it and left. I sensed the conversation returning to normal as I closed the door behind me.

Women were in short supply in the Falkland Islands. The few young girls were in great demand and often became very young mothers. Sometimes they were related to the baby's father. It was a close-knit community.

I visited Gypsy Cove during my brief stop-over. It was a stretch of beautiful, golden, pollution-free sand a short drive from Port Stanley. I wondered how it got its name. A group of Jackass penguins made for cover as I approached the beach. I removed my boots and socks in the brilliant sunshine and stepped up to my ankles in the sea. A freezing sensation immediately shot through my body, forcing me out of the water. The Jackass penguins had sought refuge in their burrows dug in among the low shrub at the head of the beach. They peered out waiting for me to go, their tiny heads ducking down as I hopped barefoot back to my boots. Hurriedly I got my feet dry and back into warm clothing.

I thought about John Anderson, now lying dead at the bottom of the crevasse at Rothera. I recalled how he and Roger Meyer had attempted some new climbing routes on the low rock faces on the other side of the harbour from Port Stanley. Our visit to the Falkland Islands had been the beginning of our Antarctic adventure and our last experience of civilisation for a very long time. Some went walking in the hills as I had done; some hired motor bikes and set off to explore the interior of the island. Others were exploring the coastline further west towards Goose Green. Mike Stroud and BAS doctor, Gordon McRuvie, visited the hospital in Port Stanley where they made new acquaintances.

"I gave one of the nurses a tomato, and she divided it into four to share among her friends!" laughed Mike back on the Bransfield. "Fresh fruit and vegetables are in scarce supply Alison told me!"

Dr. Alison Bleaney invited some of us to house that night for a party, provided that we would bring our guitars.

"I'll raid the mess for a bit of fruit and fresh cheese," said Mike.

"'Nooooo fruit … whiskey!" said Gordon, stuffing bottles of fine malt from behind the Bransfield's bar into a carrier bag. He noted the number of bottles on his already very long bar bill and proceeded to open the first bottle.

McRuvie was a sharp, extrovert Scotsman with a taste for whiskey. He could take in great quantities of the stuff. An hour later we were back ashore heading in the direction of the party,

McRuvie clutching his carrier bag, one bottle of which was already three-quarters empty.

McRuvie had difficulty in maintaining a straight course through the streets of Stanley towards Allison's house, and I heard a loud bang.

"Agggggggh!" he screamed, coinciding with the sound of breaking glass.

I looked back to see him on his knees, the carrier bag held high over his head with a stream of whiskey pouring from the bag into his mouth and over his face. He was distraught, close to tears.

"Me whiskey, me whiskey," he choked.

He had collided with the most southerly lamp-post in the world. And three bottles of good malt made their way down the drains of Stanley into the Southern Atlantic as we partied through the night.

> *Get ye a couple of bottles,*
> *Place one at me head and me toe,*
> *With a diamond ring scratch upon 'em*
> *The name of old Rosin the Beau.*

> *The name of old Rosin the beau, o, oh,*
> *The name of old Rosin the Beau*
> *With a diamond ring scratch upon 'em*
> *The name of old Rosin the Beau.*

The crooning drifted through Stanley until the early hours of the morning by which time we were either too drunk or too tired to play. Mike barely managed to strum his guitar while singing to his far-off sweetheart.

> *Your letters they all say that you're beside me now.*
> *Then why do I feel alone?*
> *I'm standing on a ledge, and your fine spider web is fastening my*
> *ankle to a stone.*

So long Marianne.
It's time that we began
To laugh and cry and laugh about it all again.

20

I found it hard to imagine the war and the occupation of the Falkland Islands. I tried to imagine the military activity there, but I couldn't. Steve Martin reported to Rex Hunt that the Argentine warship Bahia Paraiso had made a fleeting appearance at the entrance to King Edward Cove and promptly left again. I listened in as he later chatted with someone at Halley base.

"We expect them to return tomorrow," he said, referring to the Argentine ship. "There are more than twenty marines here," he went on, "and they are preparing the base for a fight." He added, "They have broken out the windows, tied back the doors and made gun positions around the point."

Bobby and Runner were still on Grytviken. I thought of the trophies, the varnished furniture and the carefully preserved Grytviken base being "prepared" by the marines for battle. I thought of Shackleton in his grave and the Elephant Seals sleeping in the tussock grass. I thought of war, Faraday and the winter ahead.

Early the next morning the Bahia Paraiso returned as expected. They called the base over the ship's radio. "Grytviken, this is Captain Trombetta of the Bahia Paraiso," he said with a clear, calm, educated voice. It had a distinct South American accent.

"The Malvinas Islands and dependencies have been surrendered to Argentina. A cease-fire is in force, and you are expected to adopt a similar course of action."

Steve took the radio but had the marine commander, Lt. Keith Mills, at his side.

"You are in no danger provided you surrender," the Argentine Captain went on, clearly expecting no resistance by the British now that the Falkland Islands were in Argentine hands.

Steve had refused to use VHF radio, the normal means of communicating over short distances. Instead, he insisted on using HF radio capable of a wider transmission so that the rest of us on the other BAS bases could listen in. "There are marines here, and they have orders to fight. If you try to take over the base," said Steve, the tension showing in his voice. "Please, do not come ashore. I repeat we have orders to fight."

His voice faltered, and I could feel his nervousness. He shouldered the immense responsibility for the other twelve or so base members who were sheltered in the church. Steve, as BC, was the highest British government authority on the island and the target of the Argentines.

"It is my understanding that your government has instructed you to give up the islands peacefully," said the Captain authoritatively. "Please check with your government," he added, expecting Steve to have access to Whitehall.

The radios were silent for what seemed an eternity. We could feel the tension.

"Please wait while I consult with my marine commander," replied Steve.

"I will wait. We are in no hurry," said the calm captain.

The extraordinary exchange was always polite and gentlemanly. The airwaves came alive again.

"Red Plum, Red Plum," called Steve. "Red Plum, Red Plum … Red Plum, Red Plum."

The airwaves were silent. The Argentines waited on their ship and the marines waited at their stations while Steve attempted the seemingly impossible task of confirming with Whitehall whether or not the two sides should fight.

"Red Plum, Red Plum come in," repeated Steve anxiously.

After a second, lengthy silence the Argentine captain interrupted.

"I will call Red Plum for you," he said. "The mountains may be blocking your transmission."

It was an extraordinary offer of assistance on the part of the Argentine captain.

"Thank you," said Steve probably even more surprised than we were.

"Red Plum, this is Captain Trombetta of the Argentine vessel Bahia Paraiso. Do you read me, cambio," his English letting him down only on the final word.

Red Plum responded immediately. "This is Web Plum to the Bahia Paraiso, over." Captain Barker's distinct voice came across loud and clearer.

"Good morning Red Plum," said the Argentine. He patiently explained where he was and the purpose of his call.

"Please wait," replied Captain Barker.

We all waited, Steve, the Argentines and Faraday. The exchange was unreal and the wait unbearable. It took Red Plum more than thirty minutes to respond, and when he did it was dynamite! "Bahia Paraiso, I have spoken with the British Government. Please inform the base that they are not to surrender. I repeat, they are not to surrender."

"Thank you Red Plum, I will pass on your message, out."

There was a silence, and then the captain came back on air.

"Grytviken, this is the Captain Trombetta. The British Government has instructed you not to surrender," he said in a most chivalrous manner.

There was a brief silence, then the noise of a helicopter taking off from the Argentine ship, presumably to wage war on the base. The radios went dead.

> *For ye shall go out with joy*
> *And be led forth with peace.*
> *The mountains and the hills shall break forth before you into singing,*
> *And all the trees of the fields shall clap their hands.*

Isaiah 55:12

21

We were left isolated with our communications severed as the Argentines on the Falkland Islands toppled aerials. Ambrose established various temporary routes to get messages back to BAS in the UK using mainly the German Antarctic base, Neumayer. However, Argentine hams jammed most of our transmissions. One Argentine ham, in particular, who presumably wanted to help his nation's cause, jammed transmission by continuously shouting and whistling as soon as we went on air.

We tried to get a response from Grytviken but were met by silence. We tried every hour for days, but it was six weeks before we were able to find out the full story. The British marines had killed four Argentines in the helicopter, and South Georgia had finally fallen to the Argentines. One British marine was slightly injured. Steve, Runner, Bobby and the other base members had

been taken to an Argentine Antarctic base before being flown back to Montevideo and freedom.

The UK ham network tuned into the Falkland Islands and Antarctic bases. Ambrose had made a number of regular contacts over the airwaves, in particular, Jim G4ERU in Bournemouth and Les in Glasgow. Jim and Les, both well-seasoned hams, also had regular contacts in the Falkland Islands. They set up a network, collecting information critical to the British. They passed it on to the British war machine. Ambrose had become a spy!

The Cable and Wireless aerials that had been damaged by the Argentines were partly restored within a week after the occupation. But reception was difficult at times due to the poor condition of the temporary aerials.

The Argentines were keen to establish good relations with the islanders. They wanted island life to return to normal under an Argentine military governor. Cable and Wireless informed us that the Argentines would allow personal messages between Faraday and Cambridge. But anything relating to our work was not permitted. I found this odd because before their invasion, we provided Buenos Aires with comprehensive weather reports three times a day, information which would have been useful to their military activities in the region.

Ambrose was elated when the young girls who operated the Cable and Wireless telex from Port Stanley came back on the air. Every morning and afternoon before he sent the day's telexes he would chat freely with them on his machine, neither knowing the sound of the other's voice. He could be heard from his radio room laughing to the telex machine as it tapped out a message from Julie or one of the other girls.

"Julie, what are you going to do tonight?"

"I'm going to dream of you, Ambrose. What are you going to do?"

"Chase a penguin 'cause we don't have any girls here!"

Shrieks of laughter came from the radio room.

"I hear that Andy from Rothera has broken off his engagement to Mary?" Andy was a Rothera radio operator who became engaged over the air to one of the girls!

"Yeah, love over the air. I like to see my guys before I promise anything! When he got here from Rothera and they met, it all fell apart. And you?"

"The penguins all look the same to me. Anyway, I can't afford to be choosy!"

More shrieks of laughter filled the radio room and drifted down the hall!

"There's a soldier at the door with a gun, but he never comes to see what we're doing. Anyway he can't read or speak English, so we can say what we like."

"What's he like?"

"Not my type. He can't be more than 16 and looks ridiculous in his uniform; it's far too big for him. And I doubt if he even knows how to fire his gun. Yesterday he asked me for food. He's obviously very hungry."

Ambrose chatted daily to Julie and the other girls, gaining information on what the soldiers were wearing, eating, how many of them were there and other highly sensitive information under the circumstances. Of course, Julie had no idea how she was contributing to the war, but he even got the daily number of flights in and out of Port Stanley and how many soldiers were there. The young conscript guarding the door had no idea that information crucial to turning the tables in the Falkland Islands was being transmitted just a few feet from where he stood.

Although work-related telexes were not permitted, I used my personal hundred-word allocation of telex space with Cable and Wireless to communicate Faraday base news to BAS. They were at least able to inform relatives that the people on base were safe and healthy. I also reassured BAS that the scientific programme continued, despite the inconvenience of the war.

The Argentine conflict seriously disrupted our work at Faraday, but never did it threaten to stop it.

"Do you have any contact with the Falkland Islanders?" John Snow of the BBC asked me. He undoubtedly knew the answer.

Snow was at Frei looking for a news story. But I was in no position to oblige him and upset my delicate relationship with Cable and Wireless. I had everything to lose and nothing to gain by giving him the story of how we used our Cable and Wireless contact to feed war information to the British. Furthermore, we could have endangered our lives and those of the Cable and Wireless staff. The question was too sensitive to be answered.

"Sorry Mr. Snow but I am unable to comment," I replied, and Ambrose was able to continue his spying.

> *Tell no secrets, tell no lies.*
> *Ambrose and his little girls are acting spies.*

22

Life on base was more relaxed than the previous winter. The rowdy animals had left and were replaced by a more subdued, introverted group — in general. Of the thirteen of us on base, nine were new. I looked forward to an easy-going winter, some good travel opportunities and a speedy return of the Bransfield — but, in hindsight, that was being optimistic.

Storms persisted throughout April and May. The dinghies were taken out of the water for the winter, but there was no sign of the sea ice forming. The air temperatures were so high that we had more horizontal rain than snow! The Falkland Island War had maintained our interest during the previous two months, and the days passed at a frightening rate. June arrived, and already we were planning for our mid-winter celebrations.

My role as BC kept me busy. Colin took added responsibility for my share of the ionospheric work. That gave me more time to organise base activities. I ran the base differently than the previous year. I kept more control over working hours and insisted on a fair share of involvement in base work by everyone. Some accused me of being dictatorial. And perhaps I was, but I was comfortable with the way I ran things. I missed my role as medic but was given another opportunity to practice my suturing when Graham, our doctor who arrived on the Bransfield, cut open his eyelid.

We listened intently to the BBC World Service every day as the battles raged in the Falkland Islands. I found it hard to comprehend that a war was taking place so close. At no time did I feel threatened by the war. But there was always the possibility that the Argentines could have removed us from our scientific bases. The news of the Argentine surrender on the 14th of June, 1982, was received with little emotion. Eventually our communications with the outside world were reinstated and our lives began to return to normal. I wondered how the lives of the Falkland Islanders had changed. I wondered if the Turkey Buzzards still circled overhead on Mount William.

Mid-winter was fast approaching, and the long winter nights had set in. We were busy making mid-winter presents and preparing for the big event. Mid-winter messages started to arrive, including one from the French yacht Kim. They had left Rio and, after sixty-five days at sea, arrived back in France. Their exploits and that of other yachtsmen continued to intrigue me. It was a time to reflect, a time to wait for the winter ice to once again set to the horizon.

I thought about Rio. I wondered how the crew of the yacht Kim had managed to live there on their way back to France with the few dollars they had. I wondered if they had met old acquaintances in Rio, acquaintances from their visit as they journeyed south. I wondered if they had teamed up with Great Train Robber, Ronnie Biggs, who had set up home in the city after escaping from an English prison. I remembered how we had planned to find him to share a bottle of whiskey. It seemed like an eternity since I had been in Rio. I remembered boarding a bus at the docks with Runner, before he got the name Runner. We were heading for Copacabana. He suddenly got off without saying a word and disappeared down a side street with a beautiful looking girl on his arm.

"She asked me if I wanted to go to a hotel," he told me later that evening. "So I went!"

There were places and experiences in Rio that I would never forget, Amsterdam Bar, Sunset Bar and a host of other girlie bars that were wild and full of drunken sailors from almost every corner of the globe. These were not like any other girlie bars I had ever experienced. They had South American blood, South American spirit and wild, wild South American girls. Of course, Rio had more to offer than girlie bars, but they were an attraction, a magnet for at least one's first visit to the city of sin.

Jamie, one of the Bransfield's crew, was a steward, just sixteen and on his first trip from home.

"Cherry Boy," they teased him.

They even fought over him! He looked as innocent as he was young. His freckled face beamed from side to side at the host of prostitutes who gave him all their attention.

"Cherry boy, come with mama. You don't even have to pay. Mama is going to be nice to you. Come and love your big mama!"

She was a Donna look-alike according to Bobby; and perhaps there was a resemblance in the smoky, dim lit room. Donna exposed one of her breasts to Cherry Boy, but breasts were being exposed everywhere. I wondered if he would succumb. Could a sixteen-year-old respond in these circumstances? The answer came later; the Cherry Boy exchanged his fruit for an infection.

While Cherry Boy had a host of ladies at his beckoned call, the ship's engineer was fondling a gorgeous brown-skinned beauty sitting on his lap?

"What about your wee wife?" Someone called to him, jokingly.

He flopped out one of the girl's breasts and cupped it between his hands, looking at it lovingly.

"Just because you love one don't mean that you have to hate the rest," he said with a strong Irish accent, slipping the girl's nipple into his mouth.

"Anyway, Mariela's my girlfriend ... always looks me up when the ship's in," he said, looking at her less than lovingly.

At that point he thrust his hand between the legs of the girl sitting next to him. The two girls smiled at each other, but there was fierce competition for the engineer's money. The smile was a message. Mariela pushed the other girl towards me, and I was drawn into the haze of alcohol, girls and sex. The beer kept flowing, and I staggered from one bar to another, held protectively by my prostitute. She made me feel good. We danced as I have never danced before. My hands caressed her breasts and the bodies of the other girls around me.

"Dance with your mind, honey," she said in good English, "and your feet will do the rest!"

I had never experienced anything like it. The girl was wonderful, erotic and, under the dim lights at least, beautiful. She ordered more beer as soon as my bottle was empty. I grew weary as the dawn approached. It was only then that she accepted the idea to go to a hotel, but I was then too tired. She had just one more task, to do what a prostitute has to do — extract every last bit of money from her customer. I thrust some money into her hand and staggered off in the direction of the Bransfield to shouts of abuse.

"You waste my time for just twenty dollars – pig!" She hurled abuse at me as she went back into the bar to look for another customer before the sun sent them all back to their ships.

Others had not been so lucky. They had woken alone in some dingy hotel room, their girl and money gone. But that was Rio, and the French Kim, well I still had many more months in Antarctica before I would hear of their experiences.

The pile of mid-winter telex-greetings stopped, and once again the week-long programme of entertainment commenced while Roy, Pint's replacement, toiled over the banquet. This time it was my responsibility to raffle the gifts. I stuffed my hand into one box to select a gift and then into another box to select a name.

"Number ... 3. Oh no! That's mine! And it goes to ... Martin!" I announced. There was a loud cheer as Martin received my handicraft of an electronic penguin. He looked at it doubtfully; it definitely was not one of the better gifts! But the standard was extremely high. Kevin, a young met-man, must have regretted losing his gift, a beautiful wooden model boat, not unlike the R V Hero. And so the gifts progressed.

Pete, Met-man	Faraday letter rack
Ambrose, Radio Operator	folding picture frame with photograph
Ian, Carpenter	revolving lamp stand
Kevin, Met-man	wooden model boat
Andy, Met-man	framed photograph of Faraday
Justin, Met-man	sealskin purse
Martin, Met-man	oil painting
Colin, Ionosphericist	framed photo of base
Davie, Plumber	brass knife in sealskin case
John, Mechanic	mahogany shelf
Roy, Chef	seal tooth necklace
Graham, Doctor	wooden box

The gifts from home were brought out mid-way through the meal. It was an emotional affair, too much for some. John resigned from BAS on the dot of midnight. He had tears in his eyes as he read a letter from his girlfriend and proudly wore a new St. Christopher around his neck, a present from his mum. Most left the bar early and went to bed relatively early, each with his own thoughts. Mid-winter's day was over, and we were eager to get on with our winter and pass the time quickly until the return of the Bransfield.

I calculated that I could have as little as five or six months more on base. The winter was nothing like the experience of the year before. We got on well. Of course there were differences, but there was a more relaxed atmosphere and a general consensus to make the most of our time in Antarctica.

In early July the air temperature dropped to -20°C. The sea finally began to freeze, allowing us to leave the confines of the island at last. We had been confined to the island for three or four months. We were desperate to get off base, albeit on relatively thin ice. One group managed to get to Cape Tuxen on the mainland, raising our hopes of good sea ice for the remainder of the winter and a good travel season.

I found the answer for Pebble Mill at one ...

Live entertainment, that's what I miss —
Songs that are not electronic,
Theatre, not dramatic amateurs,
Friendship, not incarceration,
Women without staples in their stomachs —

Live entertainment!

23

Roy was unusual for a FID. He had completed two winters at Faraday many years before and was back for another two winters! Few people have spent so long in Antarctica, five solitary years. It showed. He was introverted to the extreme, spending nearly all his time in his tiny kitchen or bunkroom. But he was an excellent chef. When he learnt that I liked a dish, he would serve it up as often as he dared. Roy liked to please and liked to be liked. He could even make a pork pie taste like a gourmet dish!

Roy and I were up early to see Ambrose, John and Kevin off. It was Tuesday the 13th of July 1982, and a date that would be hard to forget. It was, we hoped, the beginning of the travel season. They had been planning their journey for weeks and were excited when the time came to leave. Roy was up early to prepare breakfast. And I had to do Ambrose's radio schedules while he was away from base, so we were there to see them off. They planned to sledge that day to Petermann Hut, usually a straightforward journey. Once at Pertermann, they were not planning anything ambitious. As with most jollys, they just wanted to get away from base and relax for a week or so — maybe climb a hill or two, or ski up through Lemaire Channel. Ambrose, in his second winter, had the most travel experience of the three and felt confident that the journey was well within their capability. After all, they carried two weeks of food and fuel, and there was twice that much stored at the old base for emergency purposes.

It was cold, dull and overcast that morning. All three were heavily dressed in clothing BAS supplied for the climate, but I knew they would be shedding clothing before reaching a hundred metres. The sledge looked heavily laden. Kevin wore a thick bushy beard that almost hid his juvenile face. He looked serious, but he often looked that way. His eyes pierced mine.

"Are you going to give us a hand to get the sledge over the tide crack, Len?" he asked.

"Sure will Kev," I replied, deeply envious that they were going without me.

The tide crack is where the sea ice meets the land and heaves with the tide, breaking the ice around the frozen shoreline, making it difficult to pass over the thin stretch of open water. Skiing on sea ice can be at its most dangerous while negotiating tide cracks.

"Roy, too?" I added as Roy prepared to get his boots and anorak.

Roy volunteered for everything.

John was slightly older than the others. We would miss him while he was off base, not just for his good humour and keen Glaswegian jokes, but also because he was a jack-of-all-trades, turning his hand to mend whatever broke down on base. He was a skilled mechanic and got involved in every aspect of base life. I watched people constantly, looking for signs of who would make the next Base Commander. John had all the qualities of a BC but, unfortunately for BAS, he had already written his resignation and would not be on base the following season. He tucked his St Christopher into his shirt, strapped down his anorak and was ready to leave.

"I want you to read out any messages I get from home," he told me, referring to reading them out over the radio during our nightly radio contact schedule.

"But don't go replying for him!" joked Kevin.

It was barely light, and a thick mist eerily hung over the ice. They dug in their skis and pulled hard on their harnesses, Ambrose on the left, John in the middle and Kevin on the right.

"Pull!" they shouted in unison to get the sledge moving, but it held fast.

I gave it a hefty push to break it free from the ice where it had been standing. The heavily loaded sledge barely moved. But as the three strained at their harnesses, the team slowly moved north towards Petermann and away from the comforts of Faraday. I watched them stumble as they struggled to pull their load towards a huge iceberg less than a hundred metres in front. They were barely visible in the mist, and I watched with envy until it engulfed them. The chill of a southerly breeze ate through my clothes, and I hurried back into the comforts of the base.

There was a subdued emptiness about Faraday with the three away at Petermann. Winter morale on base was very different from the rowdy, argumentative winter we experienced the previous year. At meal times we ate in comparative silence and then left for our respective workrooms or to be alone in our bunkrooms. Tensions did build up, and we did have our disagreements. But there was none of the hatred and victimisation of the previous year. The animals were gone, and the quiet ones prevailed. Logically, every Antarctic winter would differ depending on the people, the weather, the work, the location of the base, and much more. BAS had the longest contracts of any of the other nations' Antarctic research bases. But BAS also had one of the most relaxed travel restrictions, compensating long contracts with more travel away from base.

I was busy without Ambrose. My ionospheric work, BC duties and radio room tasks left me with little or no free time. Ambrose's radio schedule was hectic. At various times throughout the day he had to work Palmer, Signey, Neuymayer, Rothera, Frei and Cable and Wireless in Stanley — not to mention other bases which routinely called up for one reason or another. Many schedules were in Morse Code, but by then I was well practised in Morse through regular hamming sessions. As was standard practice, I also talked to the jolly party at Petermann twice a day.

A magnificent aurora lit the still, clear night sky above Faraday. We were all outside getting photographs of the phenomena. The curtain of light swirled, danced and twisted overhead, changing its colour like a chameleon. The theatre in the sky held us mesmerised.

"Wow, look at that!" came the cry over the radio beside me as a streamer of light descended from the sky, illuminating the horizon to the south. We shared the experience with Ambrose and his team. They were transmitting from high on a hill overlooking their temporary home at Petermann. I could almost hear their cameras clicking in unison with ours. The colours of the aurora faded from shades of blue to green mixed with reds, purples and yellows. The night sky was alive as the mystical lights formed and reformed in quick succession. It was a mysterious, hypnotising experience.

The following morning, despite very low air temperatures, the sea temperature suddenly increased and large melt holes appeared in the sea ice. The strength of the ice was crucial to our ability to get off base. That night, the fourth night since the field party left for Petermann, the wind suddenly rose to gale force. Ambrose had fitted an anemometer in the bar; we looked at it gloomily as it swung to read 60 knots. I went to bed but was disturbed from a deep sleep by the storm tearing at the walls of the base. I lay snug in my sleeping bag listening to the wind howl through the aerials and shake the walls of the fragile building. I did not have to go out the next morning to know what the wind had done. Drifting snow was piled high around the windows, making it impossible to see out. The Union Jack had been reduced to tatters on its pole. Debris lay strewn everywhere. There was open water in every direction. Faraday was, once again, an island and the field party was trapped at Petermann with no means of returning to base.

"Faraday, Faraday, this is Petermann. Do you read me, over?"

"Morning Ambrose," I tried to keep my voice calm. "How's your sea ice, over?"

"We don't have any, Len," he replied. "We're stranded here, over."

"Was there any damage to the huts?" I asked.

"The small hut was completely destroyed in the night," he said jovially. "It's now spread all over the island. The wind rattled the main building and lifted part of the roof, but the building is still intact, over."

The situation was more inconvenient than serious. Ambrose would be away longer than expected, and we would have to cope longer than was expected — that was all. They had food, fuel and protection, and the sea ice would re-form in no time …

"Ambrose, I need to inform Cambridge. Make a complete inventory of how much food and fuel you have. I will come up again at nine thirty tonight," and I signed off.

Rumours abounded on base. Some reckoned they could be stuck at Petermann until the Bransfield got back in December, nearly six months away. Quietly, I agreed with them. We had a crisis, but not an emergency. And we just had to work it out.

"You ain't gonna get me off base," said Ian, "no fucking way. I'm behind these four walls until the Bransfield comes and gets me."

Ian's habit of re-packing his "stuff" to take home had become worse since mid-winter. We had lost count of how many "goodies" boxes he had made, but they were now becoming quite sophisticated with little drawers and special compartments. Aside from Pete and me, none of the others had any real desire for travel to the extremes we had gone the previous winter.

After getting the morning radio schedules out of the way, I climbed the hill in gale force winds to get a better view of the extent of damage to the sea ice. It was a dismal sight. There was open water in every direction. Some ice remained in Penola Strait, but it was breaking up in a heavy swell before my very eyes. Petermann was well and truly cut off.

I tried to collect my thoughts as I made my way back to base. There was no cause for alarm. We would certainly be the centre of attention from other bases, "Faraday's fucked up." But we could manage.

"Oh, shit," I thought to myself. "All I want is a quiet winter and to get the fuck out of here."

Dreams of owning my own yacht and sailing as Kim sailed overwhelmed me. It was my silent secret. I never discussed it at the bar. But I was determined. Stuff working for a living. A sea bum, that would be the life for me. The wind managed one last blast in my face as I pushed against the door to shut it out.

The Petermann party was in fine spirits that evening.

"We have food for at least two months, and there are plenty of cormorants and penguins around. We've even seen a number of whales, but they could be difficult to catch," joked Ambrose.

I sensed that they were jovial about being stars, stuck in an old tin hut with just the bare essentials to keep them alive. But I also sensed an air of apprehension about how long they might have to stay there. I felt the same apprehension, but all we could do was wait.

During the night the storm abated. It went as quickly as it came. The damage was done, the storm wandered off to some other part of Antarctica. It continued to snow heavily during the next few days. The wind dropped to a light breeze from the south, bringing with it colder air and dramatically lower temperatures. But the sea remained angry, and a high swell battered the remaining sea ice. It would take a long, calm cold spell before the ice would reform, allowing Ambrose, John and Kevin to return.

The Cable and Wireless aerials at Port Stanley had been only marginally improved since the end of the war. They had priorities other than repairing aerials. And communication with the Falkland Islands was, at times, near impossible — more often than not driving me mad with frustration as I tried to keep our communication commitments. But my dilemma was not likely to be resolved in the near future with Ambrose trapped at Petermann, and the radio equipment was deteriorating due to lack of expert maintenance. The whistling Argentine ham did little to help matters as he continued to jam my radio transmissions long after the end of the conflict. Perhaps he was not aware that the war was over.

I became friendly with one of the Chilean radio operators at Frei. The base was located far to the north of us. I practised my weak Spanish with him while he spoke to me in fluent English.

"Como estas, Reinaldo? Hoy tenemos problemas con un grupo en el campo — Ambrose."

Reinaldo, the Frei radio operator, knew Ambrose well. They spoke to each other almost every day.

"I'm very well, Len. Sorry to hear about the problems with Ambrose. If there is anything we can do at Frei to help, please don't hesitate to ask. You are doing a fine job on the radio while he is away!"

He had been very patient with my jittery Morse and was genuinely friendly towards Ambrose and me. But it was no secret that the Chileans were happy with the outcome of the Falkland Island conflict. Chile had its own long running boarder disputes with Argentina and considered the British as their allies. But politics were never discussed. Pinochett was in power, and a political discussion over the radio could be a very dangerous pastime.

Reinaldo refrained from asking specific details about our stranded field party. However, he probably knew as much as I did since many Antarctic bases were tuning in to my schedules and received copies of my telexes to the Director of BAS. In fact, they would likely receive them before BAS did! Telexes to BAS followed a complex route.

The radio room soon became my cell, leaving me little time for anything else. I barely managed to keep the equipment running and dreaded a fault I was unable to repair. The other BAS bases helped me as much as they could by taking part of my traffic and re-transmitting it to Cable and Wireless for me.

It became obvious that as the days passed into weeks, the field party became badly organised. They were sleeping three-quarters of the day, and the remainder of the time they just sat around the fire trying to keep warm. We had replenished the coal stocks at Petermann during the summer, but I asked them to conserve stocks and keep the fire to a low during the day. They became depressed as time dragged on; they sat around waiting for the return of the sea ice. Their stock of cigarettes and alcohol was gone within the first week. I avoided talking to them about film nights or Saturday night celebrations on base, but they knew as well as I did what we were doing on Faraday almost every minute of the day and night. I read messages from Cambridge regarding their predicament. I kept nothing from them. I sent telexes from them to their families and friends, and read out any replies I received. I kept them up-to-date with news from the other bases and any world news that I thought might interest them. The radio schedules were the highlight of their day, but they were soon to lose even this lifeline.

Their radio batteries became dangerously low, and I feared losing all communication with the field party. I cut our schedules to once a day, but as time wore on even this was too much. I reduced them to twice a week, then weekly. Eventually we only spoke if there was something important to communicate. It was imperative to conserve the batteries. They were very much alone at Petermann.

The weather played tricks on us. Time and time again the sea ice formed a thin skin during short cold spells. I could imagine them building up their hopes of returning to Faraday. They must have tasted the home comforts as tiny drops of snow settled on the feeble ice. I could imagine them searching for heavy objects to lob onto the ice to test its thickness. And it must have been bitterly disappointing, even sole rending, when subsequent storms destroyed their thin hopes.

I was under great pressure from all quarters to launch the dinghies and attempt a rescue. I seriously considered it many times. But no sooner did a storm abate, leaving open water, than a thin film of ice formed on the sea making travel in the dinghies impossible. It would have been extremely dangerous to attempt the journey.

Continual storms, additional work for everyone and the inability to get off base caused the morale to plummet at Faraday. Roy suffered severe bouts of depression, sitting all day in his kitchen reading and refusing to leave or to speak with anyone. He even ate in the kitchen. Ian was permanently in a bad mood, always complaining about something. He regretted burning all his cigarettes at mid-winter in a do-or-die attempt to give up the habit. He resorted to smoking tea leaves, which probably made things worse. Davie drank heavily, criticising everybody and everything. I was snappy and continually ordering people around.

I was feeling the pressure, and the others tried to keep out of my way. But we were all under extra pressure with additional work and responsibilities. One of the boilers we used to heat the base broke down. Had the other boiler failed, we would have been without any form of heat on base. The water pipes would have frozen solid. The boilers had never performed well all winter, keeping John busy. With John stuck at Petermann, we had limited knowledge of how to repair them. I blew up Ambrose's main transmitter and had an agonising night trying to repair it. If I had not been able to repair it, we would have been almost completely without communication to the outside world. Gash came around much more often with three people away, and I often missed my turn due to the shear bulk of work. That did not go down well with the others. But we never thought of trying to reduce the amount of work. Everyone made a conciliatory effort to keep the base running normally despite the difficulties.

July ran into August, and the storms continued to sweep Antarctica. Palmer, Neuymayer and Rothera all had aerials brought down by the gale force winds. Fortunately Faraday's stayed intact. Due to the storms and lack of sea ice there was more wildlife around the islands than normal for the time of year. Petermann reported seeing an abundance of penguins on the island, some of which they ate. A Weddell seal prematurely gave birth close to Faraday, but the unfortunate pup was stillborn. The unusually high air temperatures caused the snow and ice to melt, exposing rock that would have normally been covered until late in the summer. Glaciers were exposed, and their surfaces turned to water as they started to retreat. Global warming was on the world stage. BAS had just published the first ever paper on the hole in the ozone layer, using data collected from Faraday.

The Petermann party was down to twenty-five days of food and was running short of the paraffin they used for cooking and lighting. They complained of strong body odour. They were not paying attention to personal hygiene. The hut apparently stank because of the penguins they ate and the fumes given off by the paraffin lamp and coal fire. I grew more concerned for their well-being. We were blessed with a long cold spell of good weather. And, at last, everyone got out skiing. It was the first time in weeks. Base morale instantly improved. We caught up on a lot of the outside work that had been neglected and re-paired the storm damage. I wielded a large sledge hammer to the forty-five-gallon drums full of rubbish. It was partly to bend the tops over to make them ready for disposal. But mainly I wanted to get some exercise after the long weeks of confine-ment. The weather was perfect for forming sea ice now. I opti-mistically predicted that the Petermann party would be back on base within a week. They seemed in high spirits when I spoke with them. They had made one journey onto the sea ice around their hut to test conditions. Their batteries were all but spent, and we discussed what would happen when we no longer had communication. I would no longer be able to advise them of the condition of the sea ice at Faraday. I passed on family messages and gave them base news, including our intention to have a party the next night for Roy's birthday.

Graham baked a large brightly decorated cake for Roy's birthday. It was Friday 13th and unlucky for some. We set up food, drinks and barbecue equipment at an old meteorological store, a little-used hut on a rocky outcrop next to the sea. It was well away from the main base. We planned to have a bonfire to keep us warm during the party, and we searched the base for all the wood we cold lay our hands on. The store was an ideal loca-tion for the barbecue and bonfire if we were not to repeat last year's spectacular sauna fire.

The bonfire lit up our icy surroundings, and music blared into the night from a huge cassette player perched on the ice behind us. There was not a cloud in the sky, and it was bitterly cold. Hot toddies were served as we huddled close to the fire. We turned our bodies to the heat every ten minutes or so, like roasting lambs. The parts of our bodies nearest to the fire were scalded while our far sides froze in the gentle, ice-cold breeze. The aroma of barbecued hamburgers and sausages drifted into the night as the nine of us made a toast to Roy and his fine cooking. The sound of our crooning echoed about the ice cliffs.

Happy birthday to you,
Happy birthday to you,
Happy birthday dear Roy … oy,
Happy birthday day to you!

We refilled our glasses, scooping up bits of ice from to mix with the cocktails. We drank and played loud music until the early hours of the morning. The conversation inevitably degenerated to arguments, and Davie flattened Pete's nose, which almost went unnoticed…even by Pete. Our supply of wood eventually dwindled, and the fire began to die. We pocked at the ashes and half-burnt timbers in search of red-hot cinders to keep us warm. The fire was on the edge of the sea ice next to the tide crack. As the tide came in and the sea level rose, the tide crack began to close and crush the bottles and cans that had been discarded during the festivities. I was lying back on a sheet of rubber that insulated me from the ice. I watched the stars and tried to pick out the unfamiliar constellations of the Southern Hemisphere. I was enjoying the moment. It was a welcome break from base. It seemed like a lifetime since I had been able to relax.

The others had gone back to the base to continue the celebration. I was alone. As I lay back something startled me. I was not sure what it was. I stood up and looked down Meek Channel towards the mainland, but the ice cliffs on Grotto, Uruguay and

Corner Islands obscured my view of Penola Strait and the mountains. I strained my eyes in the dark but saw only blackness. Intuitively I felt something was wrong. Was it a flare I saw? Did I hear voices? Shouts? I kept stopping and listening. Did I hear shouts, or was it the hum of the base generator in the background? Perhaps it was the party. The faint sound of music from the bar reached me.

> *For he's a jolly good fellow,*
> *For he's a jolly good fellow ...*

24

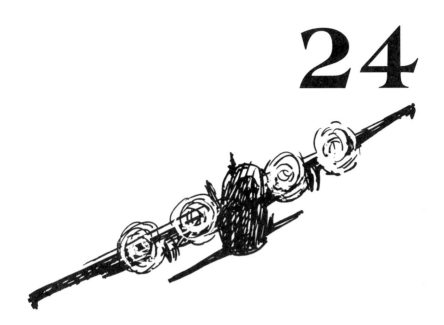

I tuned in the radio at the time for the morning schedule. Their batteries were all but dead, but I felt the need to speak to them.

"Petermann, Faraday. Come in Ambrose," I called.

I did not expect a response, but I didn't know why.

"Petermann, Faraday. Come in Ambrose!" I called again across the silent airwaves.

My heart sank.

"Petermann, Faraday."

I became anxious. I called for an hour, then on the hour every hour. I knew something was wrong.

I was hung over from the party, and I had not slept well. I dressed in outdoor clothing and skied to the top of Woozle. It was a cold morning. Sunlight filtered through a low mist. A

brilliant ray of light swept across the sky high above the Antarctic mainland. At either end of the ray were smaller images of the sun. They were sundogs — phenomena caused by the sun shinning through ice crystals hanging in the air. It was a beautiful, eerie morning. A wide, open lead of water cut through the newly formed sea ice in Penola Strait like a slice through the icing on a cake. The black strip of sea scarred the otherwise virgin white landscape. The ice rose and fell to the rhythm of the sea below. The movement of the ice surprised me; there had been no recent storm at Faraday to cause such a large swell. Undoubtedly, the swell had caused the break in the sea ice. I turned my back on Penola and skied back to base.

The wind strengthened throughout the day. By nightfall it was gusting to eighty knots.

"Petermann, Petermann, this is Faraday. Do you read me Ambrose, John, Kevin, over?"

Silence.

I knew that Palmer and Rothera could hear my calls, but they kept off the air.

"Ambrose, come in!" I begged.

I called Petermann repeatedly as Faraday became engulfed in a fury of snow that drifted deep over the windows and hammered at the door, taunting our very existence in a land where men did not belong. Petermann was silent. I shut down the radio and slept with my secret fears.

I awoke early and again, repeatedly, called Petermann. But nothing. I called every hour, on the hour.

"Were their batteries dead?" I tried to reassure myself. "Is there a problem with their radio or the aerial?"

I asked Palmer to call Petermann, explaining that I had lost communication with Ambrose.

"Petermann, Petermann, this is Palmer station. Do you read me over."

The American radio operator spoke in a clear, methodical voice. But he also failed to get a reply. I strained at the hiss of the radio, desperately listening for even the weakest signal and a clue as to why they had not responded to my calls.

The wind abated during the day, and the sun shone through the fresh snow drifting across the hill towards the base. It was a wild day, one that filled my body with excitement as I skied up Woozle hill. My baggy, windproof clothing flapped wildly in the wind, and the snow swirled around my body. Spindrift found its way down my neck and melted, wetting my fibre pile shirt. I badly needed exercise and forced myself to reach the top of the hill faster than I would normally have done. I looked across to Penola Strait and north towards Petermann. There was open water in every direction.

I had lost all contact with Petermann. I maintained a radio listening-watch in the hope they might resolve whatever problem they had that stopped them from contacting me. I had to get to Petermann, and the only means to get there was by dinghy. But it was not possible to launch the dinghies from Faraday; the creeks were still frozen or piled with heavy brash ice. The dinghies had to be taken to Penguin Point at the far end of the island where there was a chance of launching them into Penola Strait. From there perhaps we could make it to Petermann.

We dug out one of the skidoos that had been skillfully maintained by John and stored below tarpaulins before the onset of winter. It was buried below a mountain of snow, but the whole base rallied around the plan to attempt a rescue of the Petermann party. A sledge was prepared with tents, food, outboard motors and all the other equipment required for the hazardous journey. We struggled through deep drift snow with a skidoo and sledge towards Penguin Point. Every few metres the skidoo became stuck or the sledge turned over in deep snowdrifts. By nightfall we had set up a base camp at Penguin Point with all the equipment needed for the rescue, with the exception of the dinghies. They still had to be transported. That we left until the following morning. We returned to base to discuss how best to get the dinghies to Penguin Point. It was decided that Pete would lead the rescue team. Roy, Davie and Graham would be his support.

I sent an urgent telegram to Dick Laws, the Director of BAS. I described the latest turn of events with the Petermann party. The telegram had the predictable reaction. The Cambridge emergency response team went into action, and Cable and Wireless in the Falkland Islands were put on full alert. Cambridge provided me with support throughout the day, seeking information on every aspect of our predicament and advising me on what action I should take. We set up an observation point on Woozle hill just in case the field party had reached one of the islands or mainland depots. The other bases were listening in to our radio schedules. Where possible, they helped me to receive the constant flow of telexes from BAS and to get my response back to them as quickly as possible.

"Len, do not put any of the rescue party at risk," wrote Laws.

"OK, understood. We have set up a base camp at Penguin Point and will move the dinghies there later this morning. However, I still have not — I repeat, have not — made the decision when or if a rescue party will leave for Petermann."

"How many drums of aviation fuel do you have, Len?"

"I don't know, but I will get someone to dig them out and let you know. Why do you ask?"

"Keep up the radio watch and call the field party every hour."

"This is being done, and we have set up the observation post on Woozle."

I was in a desperate situation, trying to keep up with the constant flow of communications as well as trying to direct the rescue team. Roy brought my meals to the radio room where I confined myself. The rest of the base worked on getting the dinghies to Penguin Point.

"You've hit the headlines," the Rothera radio operator informed me. "Tune in the next BBC World Service broadcast."

"We are receiving reports of three men who have gone missing from Faraday Station, a British Antarctic survey base on the Antarctic Peninsula ... "

I could hardly comprehend what was happening; events were overtaking me. I switched the radio off. I was under pressure and, from the flurry of telex messages from Cambridge, so was Dick Laws.

Everyone helped get the dinghies over Woozle Hill to Penguin Point. By late morning the rescue party was ready to leave, and I skied across the island to watch them go. The air was still and cold. The two dinghies, loaded with equipment, were slid across the ice and into the water. Pete and Graham climbed into one boat, Davie and Roy into the other. They looked determined, but they also looked cold and vulnerable in the tiny dinghies. The equipment was inadequate for such a hazardous journey. They were dwarfed by the enormity of their surroundings. The water was too shallow to start the outboards, so they placed the oars and tried to row towards deeper water. The oars had to be forced through a thin crust of ice that had formed around the dinghies. The bow of the front dinghy broke the thin crust of ice as it slowly moved forward. The second dinghy followed easily in its wake. Progress was slow. The first oarsman struggled to make the next stroke. A thin sheet of ice re-formed in their wake. Conditions were perfect for forming new sea ice. The two dinghies eventually reached deeper water. A cloud of frozen vapour hung around their breaths as Pete and Davie tugged at the outboard starter cords. The engines were cold but eventually spluttered into life. Steering the dinghies was difficult. The ice determined the direction of their progress more than the thrust of the outboard. To let them continue would have been irresponsible, and nobody questioned my decision to call the whole thing off. The rescue camp was left intact for a future attempt if conditions allowed. I doubted they would. I spoke to Dick Laws.

"It is impossible for us to reach Petermann by boat at the present time. Would it be possible for you to arrange a search aircraft to fly over Petermann?"

His response took me by surprise.

"We have no aircraft available in the area. And we have no official contact with foreign parties who may have aircraft. I suggest you contact other foreign bases to see if they can provide assistance."

There was an unprecedented level of co-operation between bases of differing nationalities in Antarctica. But at the time I really did not see how I could possibly summon an aircraft to search in an area where it was impossible to land. Furthermore, there were no aircraft for hundreds of kilometres as far as I knew. The harsh environment, the enormity of the continent, the minute population and the remoteness of each base from its home country left no room for political or cultural differences. Dick Laws' response to my plea for help was going to put international co-operation in Antarctica to the test.

My best options were to try and get help from either Chile or Argentina, the countries closest to Faraday. Since I had no direct contact with Argentine bases, it was with great trepidation that I contacted Reinaldo, the friendly Frei radio operator who, only recently, offered to help.

"Reinaldo, I need an aeroplane to fly over Faraday and the adjacent islands to search for signs of my missing field party. Can you help?"

"Amigo, estamos vecinos!" he said, joking that we were neighbours. "I will see what I can do," he said, as if it were an every-day request.

I didn't have to wait long and was ecstatic with his response.

"A Hercules C-130 will fly to Tierra del Fuego tonight from our capital, Santiago, and make a search over Faraday tomorrow," he informed me casually.

It was as easy as ordering a taxi!

"This could only happen in Antarctica," I thought.

I kept Cambridge informed of what we had achieved, only to hear it repeated on the BBC World Service an hour later. We were headline world news, but not the sort of news I wanted to hear. The onslaught of telexes continued from Cambridge. Both Dick Laws and I were under great pressure. He was pressured by the press and families and was eager to resolve the problem. I was under enormous stress from the volume of work and immense responsibility. I rarely left the radio room. Roy continued to bring my meals, but most of the others kept away. I was touchy and irritable. Periodically I went to the bar and posted copies of telex messages on the notice board to keep the others informed.

A Hercules C-130 is a beast of a plane, the workhorse of the military. I admired the Chilean's offer to fly over Faraday, a round trip of nearly 6,000 kilometres with nowhere to land south of Tierra del Fuego. Their journey would take them down the long spine of Chile, over Cape Horn and south to the Antarctica Peninsula.

I hardly slept that night and called Reinaldo early for information on the aircraft's progress. It had arrived in Tierra del Fuego and was preparing for its flight to Faraday. Reinaldo kept me informed throughout the day on the plane's progress.

"When the aircraft is close to Faraday," he told me, "you should talk directly to the pilot to give him his instructions."

"Give him his instruction?" I thought. "What instructions?"

I wasn't prepared for this but had to act quickly. I spread maps of the island group over every available bit of space in the radio room. I calculated distances and directions where I wanted the plane to search. I was frightened, frightened of what they might find and frightened by the responsibility. Everyone else was on the hill, cameras ready for photographs of the rare sight of a Hercules over Faraday. The pilot's voice startled me into action when it finally came over the radio.

"Faraday, Charle Oscar Tango Forty-Five. Do you read me over?"

"Charley Oscar Tango Forty-Five, I read you loud and clear," I replied.

I thought back to my military days. I had flown in Hercules. In fact, a pilot friend had crashed one in the Adriatic with tragic results. He, the rest of the crew and forty Italian military had died. The noise of the engines drowned out CTF45's next message as he swooped low over Faraday.

"Is that you?" he asked, as I caught sight of the plane through the radio room window making a low, tight turn back towards us.

"You have found Faraday," I told him. "Bienvenidos," and we discussed the search area.

"When we find your missing party," he told me, "we will make an airdrop of food, clothing and camping equipment."

I felt confident that we would succeed. The big plane seemed vulnerably, so far from a landing area.

"Your big news," he said. "We have quite a crowd on board including the press and a television crew!" The pilot spoke in perfect English, and he reassured me that he would do all he could to find the missing party.

The huge bird came back into view, following the coastline south before turning sharply towards Faraday and swooping low over the base. I heard the roar of its engines and caught a second glimpse of its tail as it turned into a steep bank over Woozle.

"The four men are safe. I can see them on an island," reported the pilot. "They are running down a hill waving their arms at us frantically. We are turning to fly above them, and we will drop them the equipment."

I was delighted. I punched my fists into the air and screamed with joy. It was over, and we would all soon be back together exchanging tales of their ordeal.

"Four men! What the hell is he talking about. There are only three of them!" I thought.

"Don't drop the equipment!" I bellowed over the radio. "Those are not the missing men. You are over Faraday, and they are the other base members watching you!"

"Roger, understood. I can now see a lot more people," he said in a calm voice as he banked sharply and circled the monster overhead once more, again drowning his voice over the radio.

I directed him to Petermann.

"I can see the door of the hut," he reported. "It's closed and there is no sign of anyone having been there since the last fall of snow."

I plotted his movements on my maps and directed the search over the islands, the mainland, depots and caves. We even search large icebergs trapped in Penola Strait, but there was no sign of Ambrose, John or Kevin. The C-130 circled round and round the area, carrying out my every instruction. Not once did the pilot suggest giving up the search. But I knew he still had a long flight home, and eventually we agreed that he should leave and return to Chile.

"I will return tomorrow," he said as he departed north. "Goodbye my friend and may God be with you."

I thanked him for his work and sat alone in the radio room for a long time, unable to face the others.

The weather closed in that evening, and I asked Reinaldo at Frei to thank the crew of the aircraft for their splendid help. But a second flight tomorrow would not be necessary. I sent a telex to Dick Laws.

"The Hercules has left the area … We found no trace of Ambrose, John or Kevin. The weather has now closed in … The Chileans offered to search the area again tomorrow, but I have instructed them that this will not be necessary … I will not be able to reach the area myself for some time. I am very, very sorry. But I just don't see what else I can do.

I pinned a copy of the telex in the bar and waited for Dick Laws' response.

"Thank you for all your information and opinions; it has been extremely helpful to us in assessing the situation. You have done all you can, Len. I am concerned that no further risks are taken. I have contacted MOD with the view to sending a naval ship and helicopters there. But in view of the pack ice width and limited range of helicopters, they may not take to the idea. I also investigated the possibility of long range aircraft, but Stanley airport is closed. We all send our heartfelt sympathies to you and your colleagues. I have spoken with the parents of Ambrose, Kevin and John who are holding out little hope. They are taking it well."

It was Saturday night, and Roy served the candle lit dinner as usual.
We sat in silence.

I had hardly eaten in days, but I barely touched the meal.
I just stared at my plate, trying to force back the tears.
I could neither speak nor look at the others.

Nobody said anything to me.
I stayed until I could bear it no longer and left,
weeping bitterly as I staggered to my room.

25

It had never meant to be like this — my time on Antarctica. I presumed that Ambrose, John and Kevin attempted to return to Faraday on the night of Roy's birthday. Somewhere along the journey, the sea ice must have broken up around them, and they perished. I might have heard their shouts and seen a flare, but I could not be sure. The days passed rapidly in the aftermath of the tragedy. Everyone was determined to work together and get on with our obligations before the return of the Bransfield at the end of four months or so. The tragedy brought us together as a base, and there were no more quarrels or backbiting for the remainder of the winter.

The sea ice returned once again as August came to an end. But it was still impossible to reach Petermann, our first goal. The weather had been unkind to us that winter — in sharp contrast to the ideal ice conditions the previous winter. The frequent storms had continually destroyed the sea ice and left huge snowdrifts around the base. We were faced with a colossal amount of snow digging to prepare the base for summer relief, unless a major thaw happened. And that was unlikely.

I became very depressed during early September. It was the second time things had gotten to me since I arrived in Antarctica. I was mentally exhausted and drained of energy. The months ahead and the thought of leaving Faraday began to frighten me. I could not imagine myself returning to a normal work routine. I became introverted. My personality was changed by the experience. My depression affected the others, and we went through a difficult period on base.

Even though I had requested to leave early in the summer, BAS asked me to stay on base for the summer as BC because my replacement was no longer available to come south. I had expected to be relieved of my responsibilities in December, but that was not to be. I had to find the energy to continue in my present role for at least seven more months.

We overcame our bad times by shear hard work, concentrating on both scientific and base work. We were determined to give a good impression when new faces arrived in the summer, when all eyes would be on us to see how we had survived a "difficult" winter.

The Biscoe sailed from Southampton in September, two years since I had sailed from the same place. She was scheduled to sail directly to Faraday. The departure of the ship inspired us to paint the entire interior of the base and organise our stores. We wanted to get the base into good condition for the summer relief. Reports were written, stock was checked and new materials ordered. We absorbed ourselves in our work, and everyone managed to complete their scientific obligations without interruption.

I lost a lot of weight over the winter despite Roy's magnificent gastronomic events. Each Saturday he prepared the food to a theme, such as Australian night or the Rio Carnival. The lack of cigarettes among the smokers had caused a lot of problems. But while packing the Petermann party's personal effects, I came across a stock of cigarettes. I gave most of them away to the smokers but kept a couple hundred for "emergencies." Predictably, the smokers got through the cigarettes in no time at all. I kept back enough to give out one pack a week until a time I calculated to be the next opportunity to get more on base from a BAS air drop or the next ship's visit. Every Saturday night while the after-dinner cocktails were being served, I put a pack of cigarettes on the table. It worked wonders for keeping the peace; and, to their credit, the smokers never asked me for cigarettes between Saturdays.

We received news that our mail, which had been left at the post office in Stanley before the Falkland Island War, was discovered intact and untouched by the Argentines. They had tried to win the confidence of the islanders during the war.

We received news of another tragic accident while the Hero was in dry dock at Punta Arenas on the southern tip of Chile. Captain Lennie's son was crossing a gangplank between the Hero and the dry dock. He fell to his death.

"He died like he lived," Lennie told me some months later. "Drunk with a whore on his arm!"

It was mid-October before the sea ice was sufficiently strong to send a search party to Petermann. We were all eager to find out what happened to the field party. Andy, Pete, Graham and Davie volunteered to make the trip. At first light I towed them by skidoo to Fanfare Island. From there they hauled their sledge to Petermann, just as the field party had done months earlier. During the trip to Fanfare it occurred to me that I had not been out of the hut for so long that I had failed to notice the return of the wildlife. There were seal pups everywhere, and the penguins and gulls were re-colonising their old nesting sites.

Pete and the others found the Petermann door completely drifted over with snow. It took them some time to dig their way into the hut. Three penguin skins had been left skewered to the outside of the door. Inside, two penguin feet were nailed to the old, rickety table. The small room was dark and cluttered with remnants of earlier days when the hut had been occupied by Argentine biologists. Everywhere was rubbish and bits of food. Dirty pots and pans lay in a bucket, waiting to be cleaned. In one corner stood the sledge Ambrose, John and Kevin had pulled to Petermann. A door led through to the bunkroom, two bunks on each side. In the darkness Pete made out the shape of a sleeping bag stretched out on one of the bunks. It was inflated as if occupied. Pete's heart missed a beat. Carbon monoxide poisoning was not uncommon among campers who failed to ventilate their tents properly. It often crossed my mind that this or some other form of poisoning might have been the reason for their disappearance. But the sleeping bag contained only another sleeping bag. They had used all the available bedding to keep themselves warm.

The sleeping bags were from a stock of emergency equipment kept at Petermann. Ambrose, John and Kevin had left the hut carrying everything in their rucksacks, including their sleeping bags and emergency camping equipment. They had tried to make every effort to return to Faraday. It was obvious that they had had enough of living at Petermann.

I did not leave the base in October except for digging blocks of snow for fresh water from the huge snowdrifts that covered the pathways around the base. As I heaved blocks of snow down the line to the front of the base, I looked out towards the mountains. I thought about last winter, how different it had been. It was now two years since I sailed from Southampton. I had become a different person.

Two brand new Twin Otters buzzed the base as they flew south towards Rothera. We waved frantically, happy at the sight. Two sacks containing mail, fresh fruit and long awaited cigarettes were launched from the open door. Cindy's sister refrained from making the trip. Winter was almost over.

We worked hard throughout October and the first half of November preparing the base for relief before the arrival of the Biscoe.

"Faraday, Faraday, John Biscoe, over."

"Biscoe, Faraday, loud and clear. Welcome, we are very pleased that you managed to get here."

"Faraday, Biscoe, we will put a scow ashore at Penguin Point. It's the closest we can get because of the ice conditions."

"Biscoe, Faraday, I will send skidoos and sledges to meet the scow. What do you have for us?"

"Faraday, Biscoe, we have three people and some official mail."

A delegation on a fleet of skidoos sped off towards Penguin Point. They bundled our prize, three new FIDS, onto the sledges and drove them over the hill back to base. The Biscoe left to continue her relief duties at other bases.

> *It was over, the long wait for the ship;*
> *it was over, the isolation.*
> *But it had just begun, the return to civilisation;*
> *and maybe that was the hardest part.*

26

Remaining at Faraday as BC for the summer was not what I had expected. But, as EMPS put it in a telex:

"I'm sure you'll soldier on … "

The events of the previous winter brought us together. The base was in good condition; and, as far as BAS was concerned, the winter was a scientific success. The presence of the new FIDS had the effect of opening a relief valve. The pressure was off, and we could at last relax a little. Flo, the new radio operator, tore the radio room apart and reorganised the shambles he inherited from me. His task was to restore our communications network before the end of the summer season.

In November the Twin Otters finally managed an airdrop of letters. I found opening mine much less of a strain on my mental well-being than the previous year. Within the next six months I would probably see some of the people who had bothered to keep in touch with me. Maybe that made reading the letters more tolerable.

The summer routine on base turned out to be extremely relaxing after the rigours of winter, and I had no regrets in agreeing to stay on as BC for an additional four or five months.

I organised a penguin census of the local area. No census had been carried out since 1958. Apart from its scientific interest, I thought the census would make a pleasant break from our normal scientific programme and provide a good excuse to get off base. The census was a great success. We discovered previously unrecorded colonies; and, above all, we got out and enjoyed our surroundings for the first time in many months.

We were favoured by glorious weather in December, and I left base at every opportunity. On one occasion I went to the Jalours to complete the penguin census. While Pete picked his way through a crowd of angry penguins trying to count the number of nests, I took a break to sun-bathe on some rocks. I just gazed at the beautiful landscape. The weather was perfect. The sun's rays were reflected in every direction from the surrounding ice. My face, arms and legs were burnt lobster pink. It was impossible to tire of our spectacular surroundings, and every day I witnessed something new. A Killer whale with her suckling calf passed close by. Its black, streamlined, fin cut the surface of the water and sent a chill through my body. I could hear mother and baby communicating by emitting low cries. A great gush of air and spray came from the mother as she exhaled, sending a fountain of water and a repugnant fishy smell into the air. They disappeared under a plate of ice.

We left the penguin colony and toured the depots at Rasmussen, Cape Tuxen, Deliverance Point and the Berthelot Islands in search of signs of the missing field party. But we found nothing.

The summer season of visiting ships and yachts commenced. The World Discoverer delivered a bottle of champagne and Christmas greetings from the BC of Esperanza, an Argentine base at the northern end of the Peninsula.

"We are all brothers in Antarctica," he wrote, reflecting the true spirit of living and working in Antarctica.

The Barao de Teffe arrived in early January. It was the Brazilians' first expedition to Antarctica and received more interest in Brazil than when the Americans put the first man on the moon. There was an impressive number of high-ranking Brazilian officials on board.

No sooner had the Brazilians disappeared through French Passage than Williwaw, a Belgian yacht, arrived with owner Willy de Ross and crew Alphy van Brande on board. Alphy was an artist. He made the dreadful mistake of leaving the Williwaw dinghy under our sewage outlet pipe. Willy, already well-renowned for circumnavigating South America in his well-seasoned yacht, was on his third polar voyage.

"Good morning," he greeted us, his bald head glistening under the hole in the ozone layer. "We are just starting on a voyage to circumnavigate Antarctica inside latitude 65ES," he added as if he were telling us about setting out to buy a newspaper.

"Excuse me, but could you please give us some cellotape?" he asked.

Willy made all the decisions, while Alphy carried out the chores — like removing unwanted material from their dinghy.

"Cellotape," I repeated, slightly bemused. I presumed that they had forgotten to bring any! "Would you also care for a little breakfast?" I added.

"If you could also let us have two loaves of bread, that would be very helpful. You are kind."

I was not sure. Maybe he was playing a game. Or maybe he desperately needed the strange list of items. Or he was wary of asking for anything because he had been made unwelcome at other Antarctic bases. The latter was a strong possibility. Some Antarctic bases openly rebuff visiting yachts.

We gave them the bread and cellotape, and they departed as mysteriously as they had arrived.

I barely had time to do anything after the departure of Williwaw when the French yacht, Damien, arrived. Sally and Jerome Poncett, along with their two young sons and a crew of two, lived in Antarctic and sub-Antarctic waters year-round. They were celebrities in the yachting fraternity.

Film the journey, write the book and build a new yacht on the proceeds. That was a common plan among yachtsmen in Antarctica, predominately French. Two days after the departure of Damien, Graham arrived; it was yet another French yacht. There was no doubt in my mind that the people who crowded into these floating coffins were very special people. They had made a very perilous journey south.

I enjoyed the company of the yachtsmen very much, and I took every opportunity to get to know them better. They were interesting people — people who had chosen a life style that differed from any norm. Graham, for example, had on board two mountaineers who had been on the successful French attempt on Mount Paget on South Georgia, a round-the-world yachtsmen and a war correspondent who had seen the thick of most wars in recent years. They stayed a couple of days helping to deplete our gin before sailing south. They planned to join Sally and Jerome to collect adventures for their book.

The Biscoe returned to Faraday in mid-December. They had specific instruction to stay a couple days to provide us with any help we might require, presumably to replace field depots or to complete tasks in support of our field activities.

"What do you want to do with the couple of days ship's time?" asked Chris Elliot, the ship's captain.

We sat in the officer's mess, and Chris summoned the steward to pour another round of drinks.

"I want to take everyone that wintered hear last to Palmer Station for a piss up!" I replied in jest. We were full of gin.

"OK, we'll leave early tomorrow!" he said.

"Pack your bags. We're off to Palmer for a piss up," I announced as I staggered back onto base that night.

"He's off his fucking rocks," said someone. "Finally flipped his lid, poor cunt!"

Nobody believed me. But leave we did, stopping briefly at Petermann to replenish the coal stock used up during the winter.

We anchored off Palmer Station for the night and went ashore. Our reception on base was frosty, at best. We had made good acquaintances with some of the base members by radio during the winter, and we came to have a drink with them. But, for some reason, we were not welcomed.

"Go on, get another down yer neck, urged Davie!" as he destroyed a bottle of Jack Daniels. "What's up. Can't yous yanks drink."

"Hey, they have a woman on base," whispered Ian.

To Davie, and to most of the others, a drink meant a drink; and they had not come all this way to mess with the stuff. It was obvious we were not welcome at Palmer and a better time could be had elsewhere.

"Back to the ship! Palmer are invited to a piss up on board!" someone announced. A joint decision of sort had been reached that drinking on the Biscoe was more fun than at Palmer.

It was a tumultuous night with the alcohol completely out of control. Martin, who was extremely adept at the fiddle, blasted out reels in the ship's bar. The Palmer summer base commander left in disgust as we let rip, blowing the fuses out of the winter.

"He's a funny fucker," said Don, the departing Palmer winter BC. "He doesn't approve of drinking." I had often conversed with Don during the winter.

The drinking session spread to the officer's mess.

"You can have me for that jacket," announced Annie, the young lady from Palmer.

She had taken a shine to Chris Elliot's naval jacket and offered herself in return.

"Go for it, Chris!" we egged him on as he clearly considered his options.

The ship rolled under the weight of the party. It went on into the early hours of the morning. Getting the incoherent Americans into their Gemini for the return trip to shore was not easy. One slip on the rope ladder could have spelt disaster. Instead, we tied each semi-conscious American expeditionary to a thick rope. One by one we lowered them down into their Gemini to a furious Palmer BC. Annie was the last to go.

"I want the jacket," she slurred. But by then she was incapable of earning it even if it had been offered.

The following morning a severely hung-over crew took us back to Faraday. Then they sailed north on the Biscoe's return trip to the UK.

With the absence of visitors in February we managed to complete the creosote and cladding work. Everyone got involved in other work too, such as stopping leaks on our diesel tank. It had caused a fair amount of pollution around the base. We even managed to paint the old radar tower and make the place look semi-respectable from the outside. But there was a lull in the work in March when all the yachts made their way back to partake again in Faraday hospitality before leaving Antarctica for the winter.

First to return was Williwaw. We had not expected to see the yacht again, at least not until it had completed its circumnavigation of Antarctica. But the Belgians had a technical problem with their radar; and, when they saw that we could not repair it, they decided to give up the round-Antarctica attempt. Willy and Alphy organised the work on board their yacht in a very peculiar way. Willy stayed in a tiny aft cockpit surrounded by cramped electronic gadgetry with which he navigated the yacht. Alphy did all the deck and galley work, and took Willy his meals. Willy was definitely non-gregarious and headed north as soon as he saw the armada of other yachts returning to Faraday.

Amidst all the celebrations and social activities I hardly noticed that summer was coming to an end. The air and sea temperatures were falling, and the wildlife slowly began its migration north. It was nearly time for me to leave Faraday.

"Faraday, this is Endurance, over."

Red Plum was back, but this time without Captain Barker. Captain McGregor was at the helm. "We'll be with you soon, old boy," he bellowed unnecessarily over the radio. His voice was a near stereotype of Captain Barker's. "Can you collect us some of that ice that goes chink when its dropped in the gin?" he asked, hopefully unaware that I then collapsed on the floor in hysterics.

But he was correct. Glacier ice fished out of the sea is salt-free. And when dropped into warm gin, it definitely goes "chink" as it shatters. We collected ample supplies to see him back to Blighty for the Antarctic winter.

Mouse was back. He had returned to England after my first winter at Faraday. He arrived on the Endurance to take over for me as BC. His winter at Rothera had not gone well after the deaths of John and Bob. One FID had to be physically restrained during the winter because of mental problems. He was removed from base on a stretcher when the Bransfield eventually arrived there. Mouse also had two cases of suspected hepatitis and had to virtually quarantine them. The Twin Otters took out both of them. One or two others also left, having excessive strain from the difficult winter.

Mouse started drinking in the bar as soon as he arrived. He managed to reduce Roy to an incoherent mess after an all-night drinking session.

"A dash of rum with the breakfast coffee?" smiled Mouse at Roy.

Roy was slumped in his chair and nodded in incoherent agreement. For all Roy knew, or cared, Mouse was opening another bottle of gin. Mouse's capacity for alcohol was astonishing, but not unique!

Our final summer visitor before the arrival of the Bransfield was the Hero. Captain Lennie was still annoyed over his last visit to Faraday. He refused to allow anyone ashore except two people just to exchange mail. Needless to say, Willy the first mate was not one of them!

"Never again will I make a social call to Faraday!" were his departing words.

And he stuck to them, but not by choice. The old wooden vessel was soon after taken out of service and replaced by a more modern ship, without Lennie at the helm.

As the Bransfield approached in early April the time had arrived for me to pack and leave. Ian gave me his latest discarded "goodies" box. It was a strange experience preparing to leave Faraday, but there was one last important task to complete. We erected a memorial cross to Ambrose, John and Kevin at Petermann on a hill overlooking Penola Strait. We held a sermon that was relayed to us from a church in England.

All those due to leave Faraday were instructed to board the ship the night before, ready for an early sailing the next morning. But somehow I could not find it within me to leave. I stayed on base, purposefully missing the launch. I would probably have stayed another year if possible, but it was time to go. Early the next morning the Bransfield sent a launch for me.

I watched from the deck of the Bransfield as Faraday disappeared in the same sea of rock and ice that had welcomed me two and a half years before.

And of what value was this journey?
It is as well for those that ask such a question that there are others
who feel the answer
and never need to ask.

(Wally Herbert)

HALLEY BC

27

We skirted below forty-metre cliffs of floating ice that extended another three hundred metres below the sea. We had arrived off the Caird Coast in the Weddell Sea in search of Mobster Creek. I was back in Antarctica. It had all gone horribly wrong — the yacht, the dream. I tried, I tried very hard; but I did not have what it took. It was as simple as that. And then there was the noise, the bustle and crowded places. The carbon monoxide. Sexy girls and old acquaintances. I found it hard to mix. I didn't need television or newspapers anymore. It was like being released from prison or, even worse, arriving in a city after a lifetime in the dessert or jungle. I was a fish out of water. Twelve months was all I managed, and now it was like coming home.

I looked up at the massive floating ice sheet. It was a coast of ice. There was no land in this inhospitable place, and I would not see land again while in Antarctica. My home was on that floating ice. It had started its existence thousands of years before on the Antarctic continent more than a hundred kilometres to the south. It had taken thousands of years to slowly move its way down into the Weddell Sea, crushing the land below under its great weight, gathering more ice on its way as blizzards swept the continent and dumped snow. Massive pieces of the shelf ice carved off each year to become icebergs, floating islands that drift around the Weddell Sea and occasionally escaped into the Atlantic. There the turbulent sea moulded the ice to form dramatic sculptures. Eventually they died and melted back into the southern seas from where they came.

Mobster Creek, a lifeline to Halley base, was a plate of sea ice locked between a split in the ice shelf. It was one of the few locations where winter sea ice normally remained until late December. The Bransfield was able to unload her cargo onto the sea ice at Mobster Creek. There was also a ramp of ice and snow that led up onto the ice shelf above. Without Mobster and without the ramp, the base could not exist. Access to the base just fifteen kilometres from Mobster would have been impossible.

Emperor penguins watched uneasily as we nudged our way through thick brash ice under the silent, towering, blue cliffs of ice. We rounded a prominent ice tower and spotted two solitary FIDS on skidoos, patiently waiting our arrival and their mail. It was their first since the Bransfield's last visit twelve months earlier. Halley did not have the luxury of airdrops. Captain Cole nudged the ship into the sea ice to break it back to a point where it would withstand the weight of the Sno-Cats. These were powerful vehicles that ran on caterpillar tracks and were used to tow the trains of sledges loaded with stores and equipment.

The adult Emperors fled into the sea, leaving the immature penguins behind. They hopped about in a panic as the ship shattered the ice below them. Some toppled into the icy sea and to their deaths. Their plumage had not sufficiently developed to protect them from the freezing water. The bay ice was all the young penguins had known during the long, dark Antarctic winter. Their parents had supported them as eggs on their feet to keep them off the ice, incubating them with a pouch of fatty skin that folded over the egg. As hatchlings they would have endured fierce storms and temperatures down to minus 60° centigrade, huddling together for warmth. Many that could not get to the comparatively warm centre of the crèche froze to death.

We lowered the long awaited mail down to the FIDS. They were silent as they went about loading the mail sacks onto sledges. Before long they roared off on the skidoos, back up the ramp and to base. The base was quite a ways away, well out of sight from the ship.

Halley is an enigma, shrouded in mystery, revered by some and feared by others. It is symbolic of Antarctica in its remoteness, loneliness and inaccessibility. There is just flat ice to the horizon. The ice is hundreds of meters thick, floating on the sea. The base moves closer to the sea every year as the ice on which it sits creeps down from the South Pole towards the ice-edge coast. Eventually, about ten years into the life of the base, Halley will break away from the rest of the ice and float out to sea as an iceberg — hopefully, after it has been abandoned!

The ship's cranes came to life. Hatches were drawn back. And the crew set to work on the relief of Halley. They began to unload cargo onto the delicate sea ice. Sno-Cats were brought down the ramp, each with a train of sledges ready to tow the cargo back up the ramp and to base. The delicate stretch of ice soon became covered in cargo, and the first Sno-Cat train made its long, slow journey to Halley. Moving all the cargo would take two or three weeks, working twenty-four hours a day through the midnight sun.

Meanwhile a sledge-mounted, caboose-type caravan towed by a Sno-Cat arrived to take some of us to the base. This was the Halley taxi — a makeshift, wooden, canvass-covered hut on a sledge. I climbed into the caboose and took a position on one of the cold, wooden bench seats.

"Big Al" Smith (half-brother of the notorious, equestrian, two-fingered gesticulator Harvey Smith) was a well-seasoned FID who knew the dangers of travelling in a covered vehicle across thin sea ice. He pulled out a knife and kept it pointed towards the canvass roof, ready to cut his way out in the event that the ice gave way, an occurrence which was not unknown at Mobster Creek . The rest of us felt uneasy and wondered where we had put our FID-issue penknives.

There was a jolt followed by a loud bang as the powerful Sno-Cat pulled the skis free of the ice. The exhaust belched black smoke into the freezing Antarctic air as the vehicle strained under the load. It edged its way up the steep, narrow ramp. We held on so as not to be dumped out to be run over by the cargo sledge behind. The snow and ice groaned and cracked as the sledge runners slid from side to side. I looked back at the Bransfield. In four or five weeks she would be gone for another year. The only landmark across the expanse of ice in front of us was a line of empty forty-five-gallon fuel drums that marked the route to the base somewhere out of sight far in the distance.

In the beginning it was the explorers,
then the sealers and the whalers.
Later came the scientists,
And, finally, will come the developers.

28

Halley was originally established as a location for scientific research for the 1957 International Geophysical Year (IGY) and has been occupied ever since by FIDS. They carried out detailed programmes in meteorology, magnetism, glaciology, and studies of the upper atmosphere. But IGY was just a short-term solution to building international co-operation in Antarctica. The Antarctic Treaty came into force in 1961. Argentina, Australia, Belgium, Chile, France, Japan, New Zealand, South Africa, UK, US and the USSR all agreed that: 1) the use of military personnel in Antarctica was not permitted, 2) complete freedom of scientific investigation would be upheld, 3) exchange of scientific data would be fostered, 4) nuclear explosions and nuclear wastes were not permitted, and 5) all claims to sovereignty in Antarctica were suspended. Some countries, although not signatures to the Treaty, agreed to uphold its dictates. This was Antarctica, a continent ruled by a treaty. There were no politicians, businessmen or law breakers in Antarctica.

The Scientific Committee for Antarctic Research (SCAR) was set up in 1958 at the end of IGY. Its role was to promote and co-ordinate all scientific research in Antarctica and on many of the sub-Antarctic islands. Although SCAR had no direct link to the administration of the Antarctic Treaty, the Treaty respects and uses the scientific resources available from SCAR. Antarctica was a scientific Eden where there were no commercial interests — as yet.

An array of aerials marking the position of the base slowly came into view. We huddled together in the back of the caboose to keep warm. The canvas that served as a door flapped in the chilling breeze. I looked out at the desolate, perfectly flat landscape. Not a single bird strayed onto the ice shelf. I had arrived at one of the few places on earth where not animals venture.

The journey took a little short of three hours. Arrival here contrasted sharply with arrival anywhere else on the planet. A door, there was a door, but no building. There were four stubby towers that marked the building below. The base was under the ice. It was a sub-ice research station where men live like moles as the fierce Antarctic winters dump more and more snow onto the ever-deepening base. A stairway led down to Halley, forty feet under the ice.

Vehicles, dumps of materials and sledge-mounted cabins stuffed with scientific instruments were neatly located on the ice around the base, all within a perimeter marked by empty oil drums. Cables between the cabins and the sub-ice base were held high on wooden posts to avoid their becoming buried by snow. A signpost indicated the distance and direction to Cape Town, Tokyo, Buenos Aires, and other cities stretched far away over the white horizon. Sledges of cargo began to arrive. The Sno-Cat driver was probably the base doctor or a met-man. He unhooked his load close to the lift shaft where boxes of food, spares and replacement equipment would be sucked into the void, only to appear scores of years later when the whole base departed the ice shelf in some huge iceberg. The Sno-Cat returned with a train of empty sledges to collect a next load.

I climbed down the entrance stairway into a different world. The amount of spindrift snow that covered every step decreased as I descended, leaving the ice world behind. A door opened into the Tardis abandoned by Dr. Who. The light inside the musty building appeared dim, especially after squinting in the sun's dazzling light outside. I removed my boots and windproofs.

"I'm Colin, the BC. Are you a face I'm glad to see!" Colin said with a large grin, as if he really meant it.

His eyes were ice blue and his face pale white after five months of total darkness during the Antarctic winter. I was his relief, the new Halley BC.

Colin, like me, was a mountaineer. Even the sea had higher peaks than the Halley landscape.

"It's claustrophobic, boring and there is precious little to do but work," said Colin, apologetically.

Colin, by his own admission, had not had an easy winter at Halley. I chose not to pry, but BCs are managers and have to manage under the most difficult circumstances. The task is awesome. And no training is provided, not that training would necessarily help. Just one hostile FID could make life difficult for the BC, more than one could make his life hell. I took over as BC immediately, allowing Colin to relax for the first time in a year.

Construction of Halley base, the third in the history of BAS, started in 1982. But now, after three years, it was still not complete. The design of Big Al was a labyrinth of four, two-story wooden buildings inter-connected by tubes. The complete structure was surrounded by Armco steel plating to prevent damage from the pressure of the ice above. However, the ice had a noticeable effect just two years after the base became buried by winter blizzards. The Armco had deformed, pressing against the sides of the wooden, inner base structure. The walls and floors tilted at peculiar angles. Nothing was level and nothing was vertical. To make things worse, heavy ice deposits had built up in the space between the wooden base and the Armco steel. We called this space the void. The structure would be destroyed long before its ten-year design life-expectancy. Chipping ice from the void was a routine that involved many man-hours of FID labour. It was a nightmare job and the cause of much resentment by the other FIDS, Colin informed me.

Inside the base it was hard to imagine that we were slowly creeping towards the ice edge at the rate of nearly a kilometre a year. The building was spacious, far larger than Faraday. Colin took me on a tour of the building.

"In this wing we have clothing, travel and general stores on the lower level, and two-man bunk rooms, laundry and bathroom on the upper level," declared Colin as we made our way around the base.

The air temperature in the non-heated areas was well below zero. But Colin, acclimatised to the cold, dressed as if it were summer.

"Met's stores, Chippy's workshop, and upper-level Met offices, surgery and dark room."

We walked around at lightening pace. The noise of the arrival of a Sno-Cat and another sledge train of equipment was distinct as it creaked over the ice above. Each sledge load would have to be hauled by hand, either into the base or onto storage "dumps" outside. I was reminded that we had plenty of work to do while relief was going on and that I had twelve months to get to know the base.

"Generators, electrical and mechanical workshops and that's the garage," he said opening a door. It led into a massive underground garage with a long ramp at the far end that led up to the outside world.

"We cover the ramp over with long wooden poles and tarpaulins when it starts to blow," said Colin, anticipating my question.

"If you leave it too late, the garage will fill with snow. And then you've got problems!"

I had a lot to learn and a short time to learn it. Halley was a different kettle of fish than Faraday. I looked up to see Keith peering down into the garage from the mechanic's workshop on the upper level. Keith was a slight, broad Welshman with a permanent smile. He had travelled south with me on the Bransfield, and he would be at Halley for two winters as our diesel mechanic. I waved and continued my tour of the base.

"Food stores, freezers and a bare recreation room," said Colin as we climbed the stairs on the last of the four wings.

"Kitchen, lounge, bar, radio room and, lastly, your BC's office. Welcome home!"

There was still a great deal of construction work to be done in order to complete the base. Many rooms were yet to be constructed. The whole base needed decorating. There were stores piled everywhere — even without our winter stores that were now arriving by the sledge load. We were going to be busy during the winter. We had just a few days to get the most out of all the people currently on relief duty. There were about fifty of us, sleeping in every available corner. I huddled up next to a mountain of tinned baked beans, spam and corned beef. The priority work was to extend the garage ramp before the onset of the winter storms. It was a huge job. It involved excavating the ice and snow around the existing garage ramp with a bulldozer. Then the Armco tubing needed to be extended to a level higher than the accumulation of winter snow. Finally, a wall of ice and empty fuel drums needed to be constructed around the entrance so that the ramp could be covered over with tarpaulins to seal the base from drifting snow.

For the first time BAS sent a helicopter south to assist with the cargo work. At first it worked well, shuttling between the Bransfield and Halley. But tragedy struck on the second day of the operation. Inexplicably, the helicopter nose-dived into the ice and was destroyed. Only the pilot was onboard, and it was fortunate that he was not seriously injured.

The sun was above the horizon twenty-four hours a day. The only darkness was inside the base, twenty metres below the surface. We worked throughout the Christmas period, much to the dismay of some of those not destined to winter at Halley. Rumours of consternation and dissent among the FIDS reached me.

"We want to go back to the Bransfield each night instead of staying here."

"We want some time off to see the penguins."

"We don't want to work such long hours."

"Some of us want to go with the Bransfield to Neumayer next week."

"We want to …"

"They want to …"

"I want to … "

Only those staying with me over the winter had a vested interest in getting the work done. I did not exactly know who the dissenters were, but neither did I care. I had to treat them all the same.

"Listen you fuckers," I began using the style learnt from Joffs, believing that democracy was fine as long as they did what I wanted. "You've been sitting on your fucking assess on the Bransfield for fucking weeks, and now you're gonna fucking work! If you don't fucking like it, get back on the fucking ship and get the fuck out of here. I'll make sure you're on the next fucking plane back to fucking Blighty. Now fuck off and do some work before I get any more fucking angry. Any questions?"

There was silence. I presumed they had got the message. I relented a little.

"Oh, before you go back to work and break your balls — because your dead meat if you don't — I will put up a roster for one day off per person before you leave on the Bransfield. Mike, the tractor mechanic, has agreed to make skidoos available so that you can visit the fucking penguin colony 'cause I'm only a cunt part of the time!"

I never heard any more dissent, and an incredible amount of work was achieved during the four weeks of summer relief. The Bransfield sailed in mid-January, 1986.

We were alone for the winter,
engulfed by ice that moved ever closer to the edge.
How we would fare, there was no way to tell;
but there was no way out.

29

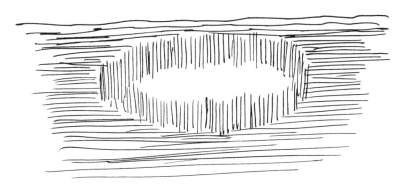

There were seven of them on base, seven recent graduates who would collect data that could tell the world if and when the ice that covered Antarctica would melt. They would help build the model that could predict world weather. They provided the continuity of atmospheric science in Antarctica. They had eyes that saw hundreds, even thousands, of kilometres above Halley. We were a geophysical observatory.

There were another ten on base who supported the scientific programme and maintained the fragile base structure. All were male, all single and under the age of thirty, and all without wisdom teeth — a BAS requirement! We had to go through agonising extractions before we were allowed to sail south.

There was nothing unusual about the day, a day early in March, just a few weeks after the Bransfield left. Steve was up

first as always. We still had fresh eggs and bacon, and I knew he would be preparing an English Breakfast, arguably the most popular meal on base. It was about the only food I missed during the winter. I could almost taste the crispy bacon as I lay in my bunk waiting for the alarm to remind me that it was seven and time to get up. Steve was a great reader. In between cooking meals he would spend most of his spare time buried in a book. We had a comprehensive library to choose from. BAS added to it every year. Steve looked after the magazine stock. There was "porn," yachting, hi-fi, camera, outdoors — topics for most inter-ests. Steve had to put out new magazines every month from a stock sent south by BAS. There were, in fact, sixteen different magazines. There were rules: "Don't remove magazines from the bar." This of course was highly abused and caused endless arguments. We all had similar tasks. Mine was the post office and chandlery; the base was officially a sub-post office. Others looked after the music, videos, the bar, the clothing store, sledges, travel equipment and so on. They were small but neces-sary responsibilities in such a small, close-knit community. One would be mistaken in thinking that life on an Antarctic base was all sleeping, eating and drinking. There was a tremendous amount of work done by a very few people. It was time to get up and get started on the day's tasks.

I weighed myself in the bathroom and added another dot on the record chart. I was losing weight. I was on a diet and, like most base members, recorded my weight on a chart we pinned up in the bathroom. This was open to abuse, lies and caustic comments. According to the chart, Steve had put on more than twenty-five pounds in six weeks. But in fact he was as thin as a rake. Someone had tampered with the chart. Some used the chart for bathroom graffiti.

Max Factor knacker lacquer …
adds lustre to your cluster!

Some unknown assailant had scribbled it across my weight-line the previous night. I smiled and dressed, adding my own little comment to the almost worthless chart. I noted that the bathroom was clean. The gash man had been up early. He had even stirred the compost toilets, a dreaded task. The toilets did not use water and took some getting used to.

Anthony sat alone in the dinning room. He was half-way though his week of fire-watch. He would go to bed at nine as the others started to work. He also had to take hourly met readings throughout the night: wind speed and direction, air temperature, cloud covering, etc. The met-men had trained us all to take the observations on our turn at fire-watch. However, Anthony had probably spent some of the night developing slides in the darkroom, a popular past time. We had had a slide show the previous night. It was a chance to show off our photographic skills. Some were more advanced than others.

"Bleg!" came the inevitable chorus from the audience as they watched the next slide, irrespective of its quality, trying to destroy the morale of the author. They were a ruthless bunch.

"What are you doing in there?" I shouted, knocking on the darkroom door about an hour before the show. I could hear the sound of sawing coming from inside, an activity not normally associated with photography!

"Developing a film," Alan replied in a voice that questioned why I should be asking such a stupid question. After all, he was in the darkroom.

Alan was the base plumber, an unforgettable person. Some people's faces are indelibly imprinted on my memory, and Alan's is one of them. He was an uncomfortably lanky young man with boyish features. He had permanently raised eyebrows and a silly grin that stretched across his face. His body had not kept up with his age. But Alan was an innocent, willing person. It required patience to understand him, but patience was in short supply among Antarctic FIDS. Alan suffered on base.

"Alan, you don't develop film with a saw! Open the door!" I shouted trying not to appear angry.

"I can't," he sort of laughed in his annoying manner of speaking. The sound of sawing continued.

"Alan, open the fucking door or I'm going to break it down!" I shouted banging on the door.

The door eventually opened, and I peered inside. He was cutting a hole through the table below the enlarger.

"What the fuck are you doing, Alan?" I asked, trying to remain calm.

"I want a bigger photograph than I can get on the table!" he told me innocently. "If I cut a hole in the table, I can get the paper lower and a bigger photo. See!" he said excitedly. He lifted the paper up and down, his eyebrows twitching furiously, showing off his new discovery.

I looked at him blankly. I was convinced that his grin had nothing to do with the way he felt. It was as much a feature on his face as was his nose or his dishevelled hair. Alan had arrived in Antarctica in plaster. Making his first solo flight in a club glider had resulted in a damaged glider, the death of an expensive race horse and a broken arm. I never fully understood the story or how anyone could have allowed him in the sky with an expensive glider.

"You see that knob just there, Alan," I said pointing to the projector adjustment control. I was less than calm. "That moves the fucking enlarger up and down. Move it up, you get a bigger fucking print; move it down, and you get a smaller fucking print. A photographer doesn't need a fucking saw. See!" I said moving the enlarger up and down. "Up, bigger; down, smaller — see!" I was incensed. I stormed off down the corridor in search of the carpenter to repair the damaged table.

"Thanks, Len," he shouted after me, laughing out loud. "Good job you heard me sawing, eh!"

"Cunt," I thought, shaking my head in despair.

I sat down to breakfast putting the previous day's experience with Alan behind me. The electrician was on gash. Dave was conscientious with his gash. The tables were laid early, and he had topped up the melt tank with snow blocks. The toilets had been cleaned, and the base looked ready for another day. Dave, unlike many others, took his responsibilities seriously and wanted to set an example of how it should be done. There were fewer arguments when he was on gash.

I scanned through the list of jobs for the day while savouring my bacon and eggs. One by one the others appeared for breakfast table. Each person had his place at the table. If anyone else sat there, it spelt trouble. Even something as trivial as this could ruin the day. Routine was everything. I had three people chipping ice in the voids and two others painting the medical room. The delegation of work was fair. Everyone had a job to do, but they had to put aside time for base work other than gash, Sunday cook and snow blocking. I was chipping with Nick and Alan.

"Be a good boy today, Nick!"

Mick and Nick were buddies, both in their second winter. Nick hated both Alan and me, but for different reasons. He was the thorn in Alan's back. He constantly goaded Alan at every opportunity. He openly belittled, embarrassed and aggravated the plumber. He hated Alan because he was defenceless, simple and incompetent. He hated me because I was a strict schoolmaster and enforced rules on the base. In fact, it was stronger than hate; he detested me. Nick was the leader of the gang, the rebels and the dissenters. I had made him deputy Base Commander to the surprise of everyone. By accepting the post he was limited. I had trapped him, but he could not be tamed. My job was to try and unite. I forced them to work in teams they would not have chosen.

"I've got Alan," he laughed incredulously looking at my list. "The fucking plumber who cuts up darkrooms."

They sat at different tables. Alan smiled at him, his mouth full of egg and, as always, made the mistake of reacting to Nick's caustic comments. He had the most repulsive habit of talking with his mouth full.

"It's your lucky day, Nick!" counterattacked Alan. Egg splattered across the table. Alan could never think of a cutting remark in response. The banter continued until I put a halt to it before too many others joined in.

There was a time when it was necessary,
when we were animals not men,
savages not civilised.

There was a reason, but the reason was lost in humankind,
survival of the fittest,
law of the survival game.

There is something absurd in the way we now are,
the way we behave,
the way we relate.

There will be a time when it's different,
when we contribute not seize,
commend not condemn.

At exactly nine o'clock I got up and started work. They knew the routine. I would be back before long to check that the dinning room was empty and no one was still in bed other than the fire-watch. I believed in the scientific programme. I believed that it provided useful information and made a major contribution to geophysical science. The rest of us were here simply to support that programme, to keep the scientific station functioning. My list for the day's work read:

Tuesday, April 1985

Steve, cook — no extra base duties
Anthony, met-man — on fire-watch
Dave, electrician — on gash
Dave, radio operator — no extra base duties
Len, BC — working in voids
Alan, plumber — working in voids

Nick, met-man — working in voids
John, doctor – painting, surgery
Steve, met-man – painting, surgery
Mix, mechanic – no extra base duties
Keith, mechanic— no extra base duties
Mike, mechanic – no extra base duties

Mick, builder – no extra base duties
Graham, builder – no extra base duties
Dave, met-man – no extra base duties
Stuart, met-man – no extra base duties
Toby, met-man – no extra base duties
Mick, met-man – no extra base duties

The three of us chipped away in the void under the faint light of our torches. Sitting in the cold, filling buckets with the ice chippings gave me time to reflect. It was a monotonous but easy day. There was precious little to do at Halley other than work, and there was plenty of that. I heard the sound of a skidoo above as it drove over the base. Mix and Keith had been out at the fuel dump – rows of forty-five gallon drums of diesel buried under the winter snow. We kept a two-year supply of diesel just in case the ship failed to get in at the end of winter. This meant that the fuel we were using this year had been brought in last year. It had been buried deep under the ice. It was physically demanding work to dig out the drums, get them onto a sledge, and tow them back to base. At base they were siphoned into the storage tank that fed our generators and provided our electrical power requirements. It took three mechanics to keep the generators and vehicles running through the winter.

The two builders were preparing for a major task the next day, one that would involve most of the other base members. We were going to raise the entrance shaft tube ready for the accumulation of winter snow. It was important to complete the job quickly to avoid a disaster. One snowstorm while the entrance to the base was exposed could have filled the shaft in just a few hours, leaving us with a major problem.

I took some time off from the void to examine the outlet waste water pipe. We still had waste water to dispose of even though we lived under the ice. A narrow steel tunnel under the ice carried the water outlet pipe a hundred yards from the base. The warm water melted its way down through the ice. I made my way to the end of the tunnel and peered into the pit. Spectacular icicles hung from the walls. The water was forming a huge cavern. It was impossible to see the bottom, and I wondered if it reached the sea hundreds of metres below. The cavern had to be monitored. Too much erosion of the ice under the base could create structural problems worse than those caused by the void. In fact, on a previous Halley base, the hole had become so large that the whole base tilted and started to slide towards the immense cavern. Our pit seemed no bigger than the month before, and I returned to my work in the voids.

It was a normal working day for the met-men, the geophysicists of Halley, who studied the interaction of the Sun with the Earth's upper atmosphere and magnetic field.

Halley is ideally placed for the work. It's only one of four such sites in the world. The data collected is merged with similar data collected from space programmes. The space programmes also monitor the upper atmosphere. The met-men discovered the hole in the ozone layer, the invisible layer of air above that shields the planet from the damaging ultraviolet rays from the sun — the rays that cause skin cancer and promotes the growth of plants.

Satellites in space transmit television, relay our telephone conversations, track our weather and re-transmit our radio communications. Space and satellites are part of our daily lives. We need to understand it. There are just a few particles in space. It is said that if we collected all the particles in space, we could store them in an average-sized supermarket! Each particle is highly charged with extraordinary energy. They are valuable and need to be conserved, even treasured, kept clean and carefully maintained. They are as important as the land that provides our food, as the air we breathe and as the water we drink. The met-men report the results of our work, and the news is bad. We have developed into a species that is destroying itself. We are tearing down our sanctuary, and there is nowhere else to go. We have set a trend that needs to be reversed. We are, to put it bluntly, very stupid!

Magnetic storms in space can disrupt satellites and equipment on earth. They have caused electrical blackouts. It is this space that the met-men were monitoring and helping the world understand. It is only long-term monitoring programmes that could lead us to understand pollution in the atmosphere, climatic changes and changes in the ozone layer. Met-men on Antarctica are important.

Atmospheric science is carried out in many places in the world, but the research done in Antarctica is especially significant. Antarctica is sparsely populated. It is a unique natural laboratory. Man-made pollutants do not complicate measurements in Antarctica. The extreme cold winters in Antarctica produce a whirlpool of air around the continent, isolating it from the rest of the world's environment. When the summer sun finally shines over Antarctica, the atmosphere breaks down and pollutants from the surrounding atmosphere are let in – an ideal time to see what the rest of the world had been doing with the atmosphere! During the long polar night, when the ground is never warmed by the sun's radiation, the lower layers of air are very stable and provide an exceptional opportunity to study the interaction between the lower atmosphere and the ground. Almost anything that affects the world's atmosphere — nuclear explosions, volcanic eruptions, lightning at the other side of the world, man-made pollutants, natural pollutants, changes in the sun's atmosphere, meteorites, changes in our magnetic field — can be detected in the atmosphere above Antarctica by the met-men. Antarctica is a scientific playground and a watchful witness to man's performance.

If it melts, if it all melts,
the ice in which we were entombed,
the ice that is more than four kilometres thick in places,
the ice that covers Antarctica …

If some disaster were to cause it all to melt,
any land less than fifty meters above sea level would flood.
The source that helps to cool and ventilate the world's seas would be gone.

If atmospheric pollution continues,
if the "hole in the ozone" layer continues,
if the current trend in climate change continues,
then the ice will all melt.

30

There was precious little to do on base except to work. We had a gymnasium of sorts, and Dale started early morning karate classes. John set up a squash league with a version of the game he invented using Ping-Pong bats and foam balls. Less athletic members took to reading or photography, but travel was always on my mind. There was a serene beauty about the landscape, and I wanted to travel across it, breathe it, feel it.

Travel at Halley was extremely limited compared to travel at Faraday. But there was one area of interest at Halley other than the ice cliffs that drop dangerously into the sea. The hinge zone offered both excitement and a change of scenery. It was the hidden coast of Antarctica thousands of metres below the ice. It was where the ice shelf began and the Antarctic mainland ended. The hinge zone was a mass of buckled ice and deep crevasses. It was where the ice that flows down from the Antarctic continent and from the South Pole, twelve hundred kilometres further south and three thousand metres higher up, slid gradually back into the sea from where it originally came, thousands if not millions of years before.

The previous winter a field party had a near escape when their skidoo went into a crevasse at the hinge zone. They returned to base, abandoning the skidoo at the bottom of the wide fissure. Shortly after the departure of the Bransfield I decided to get off base for a few days to recover it. I thought it would be an interesting exercise in rescue techniques and would serve as a useful training practice for one or two of the lesser experienced base members.

Travel at Halley was predominately by skidoo. Everything was towed on a sledge behind the skidoo. Two such ski-doo/sledge units were connected by a long rope as an additional safeguard. If one skidoo happened to fall into a crevasse, the second skidoo would stop its descent.

For three days four of us drove in sub-zero temperatures but clear blue skies before we finally found the abandoned skidoo fifty metres down a one hundred-metre-wide crevasse. A long pole stuck into the ice above the crevasse marked the location of the skidoo. We set up camp at the edge of the crevasse and organised the ropes and winches needed to lift the skidoo from where it lay. Had the driver fallen into the crevasse, he would have certainly died. I was reminded that somewhere close by three FIDS lay dead in their Sno-Cat that had fallen into a narrow crevasse some years before. They had died an agonising death, unable to escape from the Sno-Cat as it lay tightly wedged in the narrow crevasse. The cab of the vehicle had been partly crushed, making escape impossible. If they had not died of their injuries, then the three FIDS would have frozen to death.

It was a fun exercise recovering the skidoo from the crevasse. Mix, the Mechanic, was methodical in his work. He helped set up the ropes and winches to safely lift the skidoo from out of its icy grave. There was surprisingly little damage to the vehicle. With a little tinkering, Mix soon had it running again. There were four of us on three skidoos. So we had a driver for the re-covered vehicle.

The objective of the trip to the hinge was completed in less time than we had anticipated. So we spent the next few days mapping out the area, looking for possible routes to cross the hinge zone and reach the mainland ten or fifteen kilometres on the other side. It was a formidable task by skidoo, fraught with dangers. We were on thin ground, well out of the BAS-permit-ted travel area. But the challenge was exciting, and the South Pole loomed close. But it was still far beyond our resources un-der the restrictions of working for BAS.

Travel by skidoo was cold. Daytime air temperatures were between twenty and thirty degrees below zero. I piled on the clothes. I used three layers of gloves comprising polypropylene thermal liner, fibre-pile mittens and waxed outer mitts. I wore Mukluk canvas boots with felt insulation, especially designed for polar travel and thick wind proofs over many layers of inner clothing to try and keep out the biting cold. My eyes literally froze as we drove, making it difficult to see the death-trap cre-vasses. We continually stopped to check our fingers, nose and ears for frostbite. But the weather was kind to us. The sky was with-out a cloud day and night. Our faces burned in the sun that still had not dipped below the horizon since I arrived at Halley. We were well south of the Antarctic Circle, the land of twenty-four-hour days of sunlight in summer and twenty-four-hour days of darkness in winter. It felt good to be back travelling in Antarctica after such a long break. I felt at home.

We made a detour on our journey back to base. There were few places to visit from Halley, but the Emperor penguin colony twenty kilometres or so along the coast was one. But it was not a journey without risk. This route, close to the top of the ever-changing coastal ice cliffs, was strewn with crevasses. There were less than a handful of Emperor penguin colonies in Antarctica. The Emperor breeds further south than all other penguin species on the planet. Their bodies are able to withstand temperatures as low as fifty degrees below zero Celsius and winds up to two hundred kilometres per hour. They achieve this through a combination of physiological and behavioural adaptations, including a double layer of very dense feathers, large fat reserves and specialisation of the circulatory system to reduce heat loss. The male birds incubate the eggs on their feet for nearly four Antarctic winter months. During this period it is continually dark and no food is available. The female is at sea feeding while the male is incubating the single egg. When the female returns in the winter darkness, the chick is born. The male goes to sea to replenish his forty-percent loss in body weight. The penguin colony was a popular site for a day's outing from the base.

We camped on the sea ice close to the penguins. Their constant squawking and bickering kept me awake all night. The parents were challenged to feed the immense chicks. They were fighting against time. The young had to fledge before the sea ice broke up. The next morning I sat among the colony and was captivated by this wonder of Nature. But it was short-lived. I received a call from base informing me that one of the base members was in trouble at Gin Bottle. I was to proceed there immediately.

Gin Bottle was an alternate location for unloading stores from the ship during summer relief. If Mobster Creek was not available for cargo work, then Gin Bottle was our contingency unloading area. The disadvantage of Gin Bottle was that it was twice the distance from base. Unloading from there added days, if not weeks, to transporting the cargo. We had a permanent caboose located there. We packed our camp and left for Gin Bottle.

We located the caboose. There was a Sno-Cat close-by but no sign of anyone. No one responded to our shouts. The silence was eerie. I opened the door of the caboose, wary of what I might find. Stuart, a met-man who was eccentric and bordered on insane, was curled up unconscious on a bunk with a bottle of gin clutched to his chest. He was drunk. Mix started the Sno-Cat, and we prepared to get him back to base.

He had arrived with Alan and Graham, but they had left him alone. They returned to base the previous day, terrified by cracking noises they heard in the night. We made coffee and slowly revived Stuart to his normal level of consciousness — normal for Stuart, that is! I sat in the caboose waiting for him to get his things ready for the return journey to base. It was late morning, but the sun was just rising over the towering ice cliffs. As the sun's rays hit the caboose, a large cracking noise shot through the walls of the fragile wooden structure — the same noise that had frightened the others back to base the day before.

"We heard cracking noises and thought that the caboose was about to fall into the sea," they told me when I returned to base the same evening. "We were frightened!"

"But you left Stuart alone!" I said, incredulously. I was livid. The experience highlighted the terror that some base members experience when they leave the security of the base and enter an environment that is far flung from anything they have experienced before. I wondered who was to blame — BAS for sending them or the organisation for letting them leave base. And I was part of that organisation.

The temperature in March dropped to below -30°C as the sun dipped below the horizon for the first time and hovered on the horizon for the remainder of the month.

Polar explorers have to possess the very highest qualities in Man,
physical and moral courage,
endurance under terrible privations,
in terrible climates.

(Campbell Mackeller)

The days were almost gone. Just a flicker of light was the difference between a sunrise and permanent darkness at Halley. I lay
in my bunk staring at the ceiling, wondering what made me return to Antarctica. I thought about my plans and my aspirations
when I left Faraday. Where did it go wrong? I dozed and it came
flooding back to me like a bad dream. It was the day after I returned to England. I was in Poole, Dorset and turned down a
road leading towards the sea.

There were only two houses, a bungalow at the top of the
road and a large house at the far end overlooking Poole harbour.
I knocked on the door of the large house. There was a bright yellow hull in the garden. They had been expecting me. I was led
into the kitchen and sat at a table in font of a large window looking out across the bay. A high wall separated the swimming pool
directly below the window from the narrow sandy beach. There
were small boats moored in front of the house close to a jetty be-
longing to the Royal Marines.

"Many of them served in the Falkland Islands," said Pierre in a foreign accent I could not place.

He seemed to know that I had just come from the Falkland Islands, presumably from speaking with Jim, my Bournemouth ham friend. Jim had arranged for me to meet Pierre.

"This is my wife, Christine," he said.

She smiled at me warmly.

There was obviously a considerable age difference between them. Christine, the younger of the two, was extremely attractive.

"We are from Belgium," he said. "I fell in love with this house about four years ago. I knocked on the door and told the owners I wanted to buy it. Cash and this week! They were surprised and reluctant, as you can imagine, but I always get my way. That's how I became married to Christine. She didn't want anything to do with me and her family said …"

I listened and nodded, or shook my head politely for the next twelve hours while Pierre told three stories, each of about equal length. One was how his father, a successful biscuit manufacturer, deprived him of a university education. Instead, Pierre was forced to work in the biscuit business alongside his father. Eventually, he took his revenge by working for a rival biscuit manufacturer, and Pierre became a millionaire at his father's expense. His father lost his business. The second story was a complicated tale about his involvement in medicine, medical research and medical practice. Pierre portrayed himself as a medical practitioner with the help of friends, or so the story went. He told me of several instances of malpractice including one occasion when he posed as a gynaecologist in collusion with a real gynaecologist. They examined a number of women. Sex came into almost every part of Pierre's narratives. He firmly believed that he had a Ph.D. purely because of his superior level of intellect. However, he refrained from calling himself Doctor. The third story was more of a maritime ramble than a story, a fairy tale compilation of all the yachting books and magazines he had read. Pierre dreamt of sailing the high seas in his own yacht and meticulously described every cleat and porthole that went into the perfect sailing boat.

But Pierre was a warm, polite man who interrogated my every move and statement during the few opportunities I had to move or speak during that long night.

Watching Christine's large breasts protruding from under her tight sweater like jellies covered in cling-film and her long, slender legs only briefly interrupted by her ultra-short mini-skirt kept me awake, if not alive, during Pierre's endless patter. She constantly fed me with snippets of food and lashings of home-made beer, but she hardly uttered a word.

Pierre's voice became a drone in my ears, and by four a.m. I was both too drunk to drive and too tired to listen to any more as Pierre began the first story over again. I could bear no more and politely asked if there was anywhere I could rest for the few remaining hours of what I normally considered to be sleep time. Christine kindly made up a temporary bed on the living room floor, and I fell into a deep sleep.

It seemed no sooner had I fallen asleep than Pierre was summoning me back to the kitchen table. Christine prepared breakfast while Pierre continued where he had left off three or four hours earlier.

We eventually got round to the reason for me being there, the bright yellow hull in the garden. Pierre had fallen in love with the design at the London boat show and brought it back with him on a low loader. He had been years working on the hull, or rather paying others to work under his supervision. But he decided that the eleven-meter Fastnet was too small for his needs and started again on a hull twice the size.

We struck what was perhaps a strange deal. I would complete the partially built yacht using his tools while living in the boat in his garden, and Christine would wash my clothes and provide me with two meals a day. Christine, of course, was never consulted; but, then, she had said very little during the seventeen or eighteen hours since I first knocked on their door.

I became part of the family, and Pierre kept a close eye on my progress. He constantly advised me to do this and to do that, seemingly forgetting that I now owned the hull and fittings. But without his help I could never have completed the work.

Mama Chris, as she was known, taunted me at meal times by purposely wearing flimsy clothes and brushing her breasts against my body as she served the meals.

"She likes you," commented Pierre on more than one occasion.

"I like her," I thought and remembered that I had just returned from two and a half years of celibacy.

"Does she?" I asked innocently.

Betty, a middle-aged widow who lived in the bungalow at the other end of the road, was a daily visitor and also part of the family. Betty knew more about Mama Chris than she at first let on.

It was a hot summer. I got up early every morning, showered under a cold tap in the garden and worked on the yacht until late into the night. I was so focused on my project that I had a complete disregard for friends and family who occasionally visited me. I considered them an unwelcome interruption to my work that only delayed my next adventure.

It took six months of hard work before I sat at the kitchen table and looked out of the large window across the bay to see my single-mast yacht at Pierre's mooring. She was beautiful. Her bright yellow hull and fawn curved deck made her stand out against the rest of the yachts moored close by.

I unceremoniously named the yacht Yves, the name of Pierre's and Chris' seven-year-old son and only child.

On those nights when I drank too much of Mama Chris' homemade beer and was unable to row across to Yves, I slept on a camp bed I kept in among the flowers in Betty's greenhouse. At the time it did not seem abnormal. But on reflection, I realised that I was living a strange existence.

Pierre repeated all or part of his three stories night after night. He talked incessantly. His voice penetrated my very soul. I wanted to scream for him to stop. It became a torture.

Mama Chris was wonderful, too wonderful. One night after too much beer, minutes after Pierre left on a short business trip to Belgium, we started an affair that should never have been. It went on for longer than was safe. Pierre began to suspect that someone was seeing his wife, and he planned to catch the immoral person in the act.

Late one afternoon while we thought Pierre was out of town, the living room door burst open, and I found myself with trousers around my knees looking down the barrel of a shotgun.

"You were my closest friend and brother! I trusted you, and you betrayed me," he cried.

His face was distorted with anger as his finger twitched at the trigger. I felt no fear, just ashamed. This was my moment to die. The dream would not be fulfilled. I would not sail in the wake of Kim, Williwaw or Damien.

"I knew there was someone, but you … I couldn't imagine it would be you! You of all people! You bastard."

His finger twitched harder against the trigger. I wondered if I would hear the shot before the bullet pierced my body. He struck Mama Chris to the ground. I moved to help her, but Pierre reached at me with the gun. I froze, waiting for his next move and my last.

"The three of us will go to bed!" he said, to my surprise.

I was horrified. Mama Chris shook her head as she dressed. Pierre ranted and raved about our betrayal. He concocted sexual perversions for the three of us that would somehow put the whole mess right. I preferred death.

He eventually calmed a little, and the three us of went into the kitchen. We sat at the table looking through the big window at Yves, her mast nodding, beckoning me to go. Pierre opened a bottle of brandy and poured us all drinks. Night had fallen, and the lights from the Royal Marine's workshops illuminated the yachts at their moorings in front of Pierre's house. Mama Chris cooked the Last Supper in silence while Pierre painfully went through his fourth story. It was about a man who called at his door one afternoon to buy a partly completed yacht he had for sale in his garden. We drank, ate a little, and Pierre talked until the bottle was empty. Even I found the story intriguing! Finally, he stood up and raised his glass.

"To my brother," he said looking me in the eye. He kissed me on the cheek and gave me a hug. "Now leave this house and never return."

I rowed through the darkness to Yves in shame and sat on the deck. I felt alone. I had betrayed and lost the open hands that had taken me in. I was an exile. Yves rocked me gently to console me. She was all I had. I looked back at the big house. Only the kitchen light was lit. I could see the table through the big kitchen window. Pierre was talking to Mama Chris, her head bent looking down at a glass of beer. I knew Pierre was on story number four, and it would go on until the early hours of the morning. A chilly sea breeze sent me below deck to find the comfort of my sleeping bag.

Early the next morning, long before Pierre and Mama Chris were awake, I cast off from the mooring and set sail. It was the 28th of December, 1984 and a cold winter morning.

I took one last look at the big house.
I sailed out of Poole Harbour and turned west
down the English Channel towards Lands End and my dream.

32

I never had any doubts that I cold sail Yves, although I had no experience in anything other than the small dinghies we sailed during my school years in Southampton. I thought I had everything I needed. I had a strong boat, automatic pilot, radio and navigational aids, and plenty of food and fresh water. It never occurred to me to take a crew. This was a lone adventure without a destination, just a notion to head south and maybe, some day, Antarctica. My next port of call would be determined by events as the adventure unravelled.

I sailed out of the Solent, past the Needles and down the coast past Portland Bill. I sailed towards the setting sun. Sleep was out of the question as huge ships passed me in the night, threatening to crush me from existence and leave me as flotsam. It was a long, cold night; my first ever night alone at sea. I nodded off for ten or fifteen minutes at a time before again checking on the positions of the many ships that surrounded me. Their navigation lights indicated their headings in relation to mine, critical if I was to avoid a collision. I felt as if I was part of a dream.

Fear is not the word to describe what I sensed. My adrenaline ran high, like an express train. My nerves were on edge. I had been elevated to a higher level of consciousness. I knew that this was perilous and foolhardy. But this was my dream. I reached Lizard Point on the second night in deteriorating weather. I had eaten and drunk very little. Incredibly, the complete lack of sleep had no noticeable effect on me. By the time I steered Yves south towards the Bay of Biscay, the wind was gale force. The tops of the waves were soon high above Yves as we bottomed the troughs. It was New Year's eve, and I was in trouble. The wind whipped up the sea in a fury, taking the tops off the waves, filling the air with spray. Yves was tossed about like a toy. The cabin floor filled with food, clothing and seawater. My anemometer swung over to sixty then seventy knots, indicating a severe gale. The shipping reports on the World Service gave out a warning to ships in the vicinity. On land, according to the news, trees were being torn up by the roots, and a house was reported to have collapsed in the storm. I felt alone.

A ship passed close by, and I grabbed at a flare. I fired it directly at the bridge. But the wind whisked the red glow of light away from the ship, and it plummeted into the waves without being noticed.

I knew what had to be done and set to work. I brought down the mainsail, almost falling over board in the process, and hoisted a strong storm jib. I backed up the jib, lashed the tiller hard over in the opposite direction and dropped a sea anchor. This, said the many yachting magazines I had pored over in Antarctica, was the action to take during a violent storm. Time would tell.

I went below deck and shut myself in, leaving Yves to look after our fate. I curled up in a sleeping bag as seawater, broken eggs and disintegrating books sloshed around the floor. This was the tempest as written in the Bible. I lay alone in the night waiting for the end. I was convinced that I would either drown when Yves sank in the storm, run aground somewhere in France and be battered to death on the rocks, or be crushed by one of the many ships out there in one of the busiest shipping lanes in the world.

I did not feel afraid. Nor did I turn to religion. But I felt the Third Person " ... the Third who is always beside you?" I started to sing. It was a hymn from my schooldays.

Eternal Father, strong to save,
Whose arm hath bound the restless wave,
Who bidd'st the mighty ocean deep
Its own appointment limits keep:

O hear us when we cry to Thee
For those in peril on the sea.

O trinity of love and power,
Our brethren shield in danger's hour;
From rock and tempest, fire and foe,
Protect them whereso'er they go;

Thus evermore shall rise to Thee
Glad hymns of praise from land and sea.

O hear us when we cry to Thee
For those in peril on the sea.

Memories of horrible school assemblies haunted me, and my life flashed before me. Yves was laid flat on more than one occasion during the night. I was thrown against a bunk, and blood trickled from my head as the chaos raged around me. Incredibly, I must have fallen asleep from sheer exhaustion. When I awoke, it was daylight. I went on deck. My clothes were wet through, but my adrenaline was too high to feel the cold. I looked around to see if I was in imminent danger, half expecting to see a cliff looming overhead. But there was open sea in all directions. The storm had abated, but the sea was still angry. The rigging was damaged, but I had survived the savage ordeal. I reckoned my position by estimating wind strength and direction and decided that I had been blown towards the Channel Islands and the northern coast of France.

The wind had turned to the south but was still blowing hard. To continue my journey south was impossible. Yves was damaged and would need repair. I made the decision to head in the direction of Plymouth for repairs and to reconsider the wisdom of what I was doing! I had no charts for Plymouth, and Yves was difficult to manage with the broken rigging.

"Mayday, mayday," I called over the VHF emergency frequency, not knowing if the radio had survived the water damage.

I felt ashamed that I needed help. But without it my yacht and I were unlikely to survive another day. I considered sinking Yves close to a beach, rowing ashore and inventing some face-saving story; then I could forget the whole silly saga. My call was answered.

"Vessel calling on this frequency, please make yourself known. This is the Plymouth Coast Guard, over."

I looked at the radio. Perhaps I could make it alone. There was a long silence.

"Vessel calling on this frequency, please make yourself known. This is the Plymouth Coast Guard. I repeat, this is the Plymouth Coast Guard, over."

"Plymouth Coast Guard, this is the yacht Yves... ."

Using direction-finding equipment, they checked my position and informed me that my navigation was spot-on; I was heading directly for Plymouth. But the decision to call out the lifeboat had to be mine, they informed me.

"Are you requesting the assistance of the Plymouth lifeboat?" the Coast Guard asked.

I hesitated, but why die for the sake of my pride.

The lifeboat came alongside in an appalling sea. A crew member made a perilous leap from the lifeboat onto Yves. He immediately took charge of the situation and secured the flapping rigging and attached a towline from the lifeboat.

"Like something to eat?" He asked, unzipping his dry suit to get out a can of self-heating soup.

I was taken aback by what I saw.

"Don't worry about the dog collar," he said. "I've not come here to preach, but you caught me in the middle of my church service when I was called out!"

The hymn rang through my head.

O hear us when we cry to Thee
For those in peril on the sea.

I had been rescued on New Year's Day, 1985.

My ego was dented. The big plan had failed. I had taken on more than I could chew, but I was not to be beaten. I repaired Yves the following day and sailed back to Southampton in strong winds and a following sea. It was nearly three months before I tried again, but try again I did.

Spring was in the air as I sailed out of Southampton into the English Channel, passing The Needles at the most westerly tip of the Isle of Wight for the second time. My experience was behind me, my boat was stronger and I had the experience of surviving a terrifying gale in one of the most feared shipping channels in the world. With greater confidence than before I turned south at Lands End.

The feared Bay of Biscay was good to me. I was at one with Yves in light winds and beautiful blue skies. Dolphins accompanied me, and even the whales gave me a passing glance. I slept on deck and went below only to prepare food. A pigeon spent a night next to the mast, taking an interlude from its racing duties. Alone at sea the silence was beautiful — an alluring experience that can only be compared with being alone in the mountains.

But the sea is not good all of the time. I remembered reading about the fog in a magazine, but it had completely slipped my mind. I passed the northern tip of Portugal and corrected my course down the West Coast. Before long I was in thick fog that lasted day and night. I was so far off the coast that navigation was relatively unimportant. But the area was infested with ships, ships making the same journey. And there were fishing boats and whatever else was hidden behind the thick blanket that swirled around me. I was in prime fishing grounds. I knew they were there because I could hear them. The sound of their engines carried through the fog. It was terrifying. I had no radar, and it was unlikely that radar on other ships would detect a boat as tiny as Yves. There was no reference point. I peered into the fog but had no idea if I could see a few metres or a kilometre. I expected a large hull to loom towards me at any moment and send Yves and me to the bottom of the sea without a trace.

I don't remember how many days I was in the fog, but my nerves were shattered at the end of it. I had no maps of Lisbon, but I decided to put into port. I needed a rest, a break from this adventure. I had lost confidence. I had been at sea nearly two weeks and had eaten and slept very little. I had many things to learn, not the least of which was how to arrive in a foreign port.

I stayed in Lisbon just two days. There was no point in staying longer. I have to admit being frightened as I sailed out of port. I again headed south and towards Cape Vincent. Africa lay ahead. South America and the Atlantic were to the right and the Mediterranean to the left. I had reached a turning point in my life. I had the dream. If you don't have a dream, how could you have a dream come true? I had re-stocked my water supply. I had plenty of food. I had no reason not to set the self-steering for

Rio and on to the Falkland Islands and Antarctica. How long would it take me – six weeks, eight weeks?

I felt confident that I could make it.
"Turn right, starboard," echoed a voice in my head
the wind tugged at Yves´ sails as if to give me encouragement
the Atlantic, South America — I knew the way,
I looked long and hard to the West,
I looked long and hard into my soul;
I headed East into the Mediterranean.

33

We gathered on top of the base for the event. It was a turning point, a milestone in our calendar. Hot toddies were served to keep out the cold. But it was bitterly cold; the sun was low on the horizon, barely visibly through a haze of frozen ice crystals. We stamped about trying to keep our feet warm while waiting, banging our mitts together as our fingers froze. We exhaled mists of ice that hung suspended in front of our faces in the still air. We knew that the five months ahead would be different. Each of us had to find a way to cope with the change.

At the predicted hour the sun dropped below the frozen, featureless horizon. We raised our glasses as it disappeared in a final twinkle, taking with it our long shadows and leaving us in darkness. It was like losing an old friend — someone I was used to seeing every morning, but one day was not there. The sun was gone and would not return in the morning. The next sunrise would be in five months.

Those five dark months of mole-like existence under the ice were enough to change any man. There was nothing else to do but work, read, eat, drink and sleep — and the odd bit of partying at any excuse. I was in my third Antarctic winter, and my personality had changed over the years with the constant isolation. I had become more insular and introverted than at Faraday. I was potentially a recluse. Had I not had the responsibility of running the base, I would have avoided all personal contact with the other base members. Mealtimes became painful. It became difficult to socialise, even to sit with the others. I became hard, strict and isolated in my capacity as BC.

"He won't keep it up all winter! The fucker will crack up!" said Nick behind my back, relentless in his aggression.

It mattered little that he loathed me, but I despised his melee of verbal abuse at every mealtime. He was always trying to destroy someone, usually Alan or Graham. He provoked them, goading them into saying something, anything. And then, if they were foolish enough to make a comment, he'd set upon them with his sick banter. Some of the others joined in so as not to be seen as critical of the ill treatment. Alan's and Graham's lives were hell.

The silence at mealtimes was almost as bad as the mockery. The sound of cutlery on the plates was uncomfortably loud. Someone would giggle, and someone would whisper "shhh ..." Someone would whisper a cutting remark, just loud enough for the person it was aimed at to hear. It was explosive. The outcome was uncertain. Sometimes it passed, and sometimes it ignited. Meals were to be eaten quickly and left, and another day was done.

As I listened to Nick's verbal abuse of Alan and Graham, I wondered
did EMPS ask him the same question,
"Why do you want to go to Antarctica?"
And if so, how did he reply?

34

The first runner exited the garage ramp at nine a.m. I was about fourth. Keith was just in front of me, stumbling in a drift of snow as a crust of ice gave way under his weight. He left a trail of frozen vapour like a high altitude jet. The cold was intense. I puffed my way round the base in the darkness, in temperatures touching minus fifty degrees Centigrade. It was a life or death run. I felt the freezing air penetrate my lungs as I gasped, passing the halfway point under the met-tower, wondering if I

would be able to make the second half of the run and get back into the warmth. I feared falling into the snow; my body would have instantly frozen like freeze-dried potatoes. I was naked, as were all the runners. The mid-winter streak was a tradition at Halley. Mukluk boots were the only item of clothing permitted. The lights around the base illuminated Keith's naked body as he passed in a haze of frozen breath. My limbs began to tighten in the cold, and my legs felt heavy as I stumbled on. I was encouraged by the thought of a warm blanket and hot toddies that were waiting upon my return at the bottom of the garage ramp.

As I neared the ramp I saw Dale at the start of his run. His face was red with exertion even before he started. He had been up all night celebrating the start of mid-winter with his frequent drinking partners, Keith and Mike. They had formed a good friendship over the winter. All three of them were in their first year at Halley and easily managed the trials and tribulations of base life. They were a good crew, and it was fun to winter with them.

"Morning Dale!" I called out, feeling pleased with myself at almost completing my circuit.

He looked up to see who it was and stumbled, face down into the snow.

"Shit!" he uttered.

They were possibly his last words. He was covered in snow and in trouble. He had almost the complete circuit still to run. I was too cold to worry about him. I dived into the ramp and ran down for my hot toddy and blanket. For me, the first event of mid-winter's day was over and a week of familiar celebration lay ahead. The tradition had gone on for generations of Antarctic explorers.

With the twenty-four-hour winter nights came the southern aurora. The colder the night and the greater the ionospheric activity, the better was the aurora. Curtains of light swept across the night sky. The aurora's colours rapidly changed from crimson reds to greens and blues. The clouds of light formed and reformed in ever-changing shapes. Bright stars penetrated the spectacular displays like background to an artist's mural. They were impressive sights, marred only by the bitter cold that had to be endured in order to watch them. The Union Jack, frozen on its flagpole over the base, provided the foreground in sharp contrast to the continuously changing patterns of light flickering above. It was impossible to tire of watching the aurora, but patience was required to get the best sightings. The mind always hoped that the next changing pattern would climax better than the one before. But eventually the cold drove us back into the base.

"God, you missed a beauty. The sky lit up like a bonfire. A real, fucking blazer of aurora!" was the frequent message to the lazy ones and those who were indifferent to the natural beauties of Antarctica.

We endured the long Antarctic winter as many had done before us. Many had done it without the comforts of a base supplied by an organisation like BAS. Everyone tried to complete their work as best they could, carrying out their responsibilities with a sense of pride and obligation. Personal differences and moods never got in the way of completing our scientific objectives. Much of the responsibility for ensuring a successful winter lay with me, the BC. It was hard to compare the overall success or failure of one winter with another. But, from afar, BAS monitored closely events on their bases. The long dark winter months passed slowly and monotonously.

Eventually the time came that we had all been waiting for. Everyone gathered on top of the tubes for hot toddies, as we had done five months before, each with a camera slung round his neck. We stamped about trying to keep warm. Each of us had coped with the winter seclusion in his own way. At the predicted hour the sun peeked above the frozen, featureless horizon; and our long shadows returned. The five months of darkness was behind us. We raised our glasses to welcome the twinkle of sunlight that sent a magnificent warmth into the very heart of our souls.

I was so long on ice,
I became like ice.

35

"This is the BBC World News, Saturday 2nd of November 1986. The Footsteps of Scott Expedition left today for its attempt to reach the South Pole by following the same route as Scott on his fatal expedition to be the first man to reach the south pole in 1911…. Bob Swan and …"

As the spring dawn awakened Antarctica, the adventurers, tourists and summer visitors were making ready for their journeys. Most visits had been prepared for months, even years. The news took me by surprise, but with admiration for their effort. Swan had started his dream, to walk to the South Pole. Mike Stroud was back as expedition doctor, and Roger Mear was there too. It was the beginning of the summer season, the "silly season." Of course, few of us thought that they would make it. On the contrary, I thought that their chances of following Scott's footsteps were extremely high … that they would die somewhere close to where Scott had died and where he still lies entombed in the ice that is slowly making its way to the ice edge. I wondered how many more years it would be before Scott and his compatriots floated out to sea, still at peace in their tent embedded in an iceberg.

But Swan was following in the footsteps of a long and distinguished British tradition of Antarctic exploration that began when Captain Cook circumnavigated the continent in 1775. During his circumnavigation he discovered South Georgia and wrote "Should anyone posses the resolution and the fortitude to elucidate this point by pushing yet further south than I have done, I should not envy him the fame of his discovery, but I make bold to declare that the world will not derive benefit from it." When Cook returned to England with tales of great seal populations, the sealers were then working against a depleting seal population in the northern arctic regions. They quickly set their sights on the southern waters. The sealers and whalers played a major part in exploration of the southern continent.

Scientific interest in Antarctica commenced when James Ross set sail for Antarctica in 1840 with an interest in biology and physics. But not until Scott's expedition in 1901 was there a serious attempt to explore the interior of the continent. On that expedition he discovered the Transantarctic Mountains. From his expeditions to Antarctica Scott accumulated a mass of scientific information.

Shackleton was a member of Scott's 1901 expedition but, ironically, was sent back to England after the first year as unfit to continue. Shackleton must have been as disappointed as Scott when he heard that the Norwegian, Amunsden, had reached the South Pole on the 14th December, 1911. For Scott it was the final blow when he reached the South Pole, just a few days after Amunsden, and found a tent that Amunsden had abandoned as proof of being the first man to step foot on the bottom of the world. Shackleton vowed to return to Antarctica and set off in 1914 to cross the continent. But he was defeated just 100 miles short of the South Pole. In 1921, five years after the end of his

Transantarctic expedition, he returned to circumnavigate Antarctica. This voyage ended in his historic shipwreck when his vessel, the Endurance, was crushed by ice. He managed to reach a small island, Elephant Island. He survived a winter on the tiny island with few provisions and his full complement of crew. The following summer he made a remarkable escape in a small boat to South Georgia.

In 1925 the Falkland Islands Dependencies Government set up the first British research station on South Georgia using revenue collected from the lucrative whaling industry, which was based on the island. This initiated a new era of Antarctic exploration. In 1944 the Colonial Office established the first station in Antarctica under the organisation of the Falkland Islands Dependencies Survey (FIDS), which later became BAS. The first station was at Station A, or Port Lockroy as it became known, where the first ionospheric measurements were taken in Antarctica. This work was later transferred to Faraday when Port Lockroy was closed in 1962. FIDS and BAS developed a comprehensive scientific programme in Antarctica, a programme that has continued until the present day.

Others made their way to Antarctica, but on a smaller scale. One ex-FID had set up a tourist camp on the Ross Ice shelf on the far side of the continent. For a fee, tourists could fly there from New Zealand to brave the continent's harsh environment at a makeshift camp. Some ventured from this camp on private adventures. A Japanese motorcyclist attempted to drive to the South Pole. A Japanese mountaineer tried a solo climb of Mt. Erebus, Antarctica's highest mountain at 4,000 metres. But many tourists paid the price for risky tourism. One flight to Mt. Erebus ended in disaster when the plane crashed into the mountainside.

The number of people wishing to visit Antarctica is likely increase. Many will bring their own brand of transport — balloons, canoes, hang-gliders, micro-lights, windsurfing boards or even hovercraft. Each will have an impact; each will change the continent forever.

The winter population of Antarctica barely exceeded four or five hundred people on about twenty-five permanently manned bases scattered around the fourteen million square kilometres of ice and land. That was one person per 28,000 square kilometres. Even in summer there was room to breathe! However, there has never been a self-sufficient colony on the continent. There was no indigenous population. When the winter dawn set, expeditions, yachtsmen, tourist ships, fishing vessels, aircraft and summer visitors all left. Only those brave few wintered to maintain the scientific programmes.

Swan made his walk. He was the first man to walk to both poles. Stroud formed an expedition with Ranulph Fiennes, and they went on to be the first men to walk across the continent. Others will follow with their own "firsts," each in search of his or her adventure, for his or her own reason.

Antarctica will remain in the focus of nations, not just for scientific reasons, but also for what unknown minerals may lie beneath the ice. Some day, icebergs may be captured and towed to warmer climates where water is in shortage. Antarctica is protected from developers, but only while development is uneconomical. As yet, only coal could be exploited. Great coal seams extend to the surface, but the cost of extracting it would be prohibitive.

Antarctica is governed by political utopia. All that we know of a government and countries outside Antarctica can be forgotten. There are no Antarctic politicians to elect, no Antarctic municipal offices to decree how people on the continent should run their lives, and no boarder guards to check passports. Anyone can set foot on Antarctica. The world was like this before it became divided and segregated by "owners" of the land who raised flags and formed armies to protect what was claimed as theirs. A treaty, a pact between nations, governs Antarctica. For now, at least, the Antarctic Treaty works; and all territorial claims are frozen — but not dead.

I claim this land as mine,
to the horizon in every direction,
to the mountains that lie to the north
and the river and sea to the south.

This is our flag, and this is our country.
You will live under this flag, and my armies will protect you.
You will be safe and have a better life.
And I believed him.
Even when he grew rich and I poor,
I believed him.

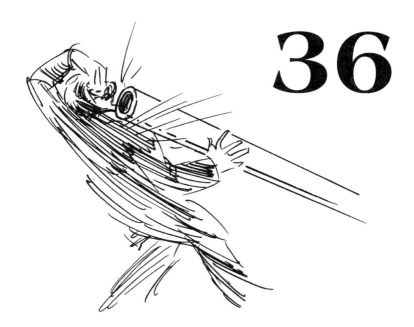

36

I had hoped for something more. I wanted one last journey across the hinge and into the interior, to the Theron Mountains or the Shackleton Range just 300 kilometres away. Or I'd venture to our nearest neighbours, a German base 600 kilometres away. Or maybe I'd even take a quick blast to the South Pole 1,200 kilometres due south. But it was not to be; I was not to leave base again until the Bransfield called many months later.

I ducked into the bottom of the service shaft, a narrow vertical shaft adjacent to the main stairwell. It contained the conduit that vented fumes from the kitchen's Aga cookers. The conduit vented the aroma of freshly baked bread over the surrounding ice. We had completed extending the shaft after the winter storms. It was an arduous task in the freezing conditions. Graham and Alan were working on extending the vent pipe from the cookers and were on a narrow platform high up inside the shaft. I was lending a helping hand. I tied another heavy pipe to the haul rope and left the shaft. They pulled the pipe up and stored it on the ledge next to the other pipes they were about to install. The days were getting longer, and there was still a lot of base work to do before the return of the Bransfield. Every available person was lending a hand somewhere to help with the workload. I poked my head back into the shaft.

"Just one more," I shouted and climbed back in to tie on the last pipe. I could barely see them in the dim light above. Their breath turned to mist in the cold air. "OK, take her up," I called.

I had left the narrow service shaft each time a pipe was raised. This was the last pipe.

"How's it going, Graham? Need anything else?" I called as they untied the pipe.

"No, that's fine. Thanks for your help, Len!"

I looked around the shaft to see what work was outstanding. It was a question of pride to have accomplished all the outstanding base work and have the base ready for the incoming crew. This was my role, to ensure that the base was maintained in order to enable the scientific work to continue.

"Look out!" Graham screamed from above.

In the darkness I could just see a pipe tumble from the ledge. There was no time to duck out of the low entrance to the shaft, so I held my arms tightly over my head for protection. There was a silence, and then the pipe bounced off my right shoulder. I felt my collar bone collapse under the impact. Had it hit my head, I would have been dead. If a second pipe fell, I might not be so lucky. Instinctively, I somehow managed to duck out of the shaft before any more pipes came down. I knew that my shoulder had been shattered, and I staggered towards the surgery room. Ironically, John was giving Dale a first aid class. The pain was excruciating. I lay on the floor, fearing that I was going to pass out. John erected the x-ray machine over my horizontal body.

"Broken in four places," he informed me, examining the x-rays. "You won't be going anywhere for a while."

There were to be no more "jollies," no more trips away from base and no more skiing around at high speeds behind a skidoo. My adventure had come to an end except for spending a few months working about base like an injured bird with a broken wing.

As a young man I had lived and worked on Unst in the Shetland Isles north of the Scottish mainland. I grew to love the isolation of the island after the pace of city life. I was happy on Unst. I read prolifically, mainly books on the Arctic and Antarctic. Shackleton was my hero, but many others had written accounts of polar adventures that took me beyond reality. I dreamt of one day being able to go to Antarctica. I returned to the city, studied and became a teacher of mathematics. But the dream of Antarctica never left. The best way for me to get to Antarctica was to secure employment with BAS. I was a mountaineer and an experienced adventurer, but I did not mix in circles where there was the possibility of an adventure south. It was EMPS and BAS that gave me the best alternative. My adventure had taken me through three Antarctic winters, and the time had come to prepare for my final journey north.

Antarctica, a place of extremes. It is the fifth largest and highest of all the continents. It is one of the world's last great wildernesses, virtually untouched by man's activities. Antarctica was the last continent discovered by man. It is still the least known about. The surface of the moon is better mapped than parts of Antarctica. Because of its isolation and extreme climate, Antarctica has a special, natural beauty.

Some abhor isolation while others thrive on it. For some, essentials of every day life are televisions, telephones, shopping, family, restaurants, pubs and nightclubs. For others, none of these are necessary and a life free of politics and financial concerns is bliss. Bases in Antarctica have good, bad and mediocre years. The base members themselves determine quality; one misfit is common and can be managed, but two can shatter the harmony.

On Antarctica may or may not reflect life on bases administered by other countries, or even other seasons in Antarctica with BAS. Whatever the organisation, whatever the reason for visiting Antarctica and whatever the experience, each person that leaves Antarctica leaves a changed person.

The days grew ever longer until, in August, the midnight sun once again shone over Halley. The long months of winter storms eventually came to an end, and we emerged from our sub-ice station like animals after hibernation. The tension caused by our confinement evaporated. One group headed off in the direction of the Emperor penguin colony. Another went towards the hinge zone, leaving the remainder to race around on skis towed behind a skidoo. My arm grew stronger, and I was able to enjoy some minor skiing excursions.

Antarctica is not a place to live; it is a place to visit. Those who leave before they reach their goals are drawn to return again, and again until they succeed. I was. Even now, years later, Antarctica lives on in my mind. It is as much a part of me as the place where I was born.

The day came sooner than expected, and before I was ready. It was over and could not be repeated. Antarctica was not out of my blood, but neither could I go on living in such extreme isolation. I shaved my beard and cut my hair. It had been a long time since I examined myself. I looked older. I moved slower, and my movements were more pronounced than before. I was not the same person as the one who had come to Antarctica.

I would leave Antarctica and go … my lips mouthed the word "home." But I had no home. I would just leave Antarctica and turn up someplace else as someone else. I would buy a car, go back to teaching and play squash in the evening before a quiet drink in the local pub. I knew they would ask.

"Haven't seen you in a while, Len. How's you been?"

And I would reply. "Oh, I just haven't been out much lately. You know how it is … a lot of work." How could they understand?

I would sip my beer, reflect and watch the man in the corner not talking to his wife. He would probably not even know where Antarctica was, even if I told him.

"Really," he would probably say, disinterested. "All that foreign food and polar bears. I saw a programme about that once. You know, the natives living like animals. Fascinating stuff," and his wife would nod, relieved that the silence between them had been broken. She would check her watch to see how long it would be before she could go home to bed.

I stood alone on deck as the Bransfield carried me northwards, away from Halley. A hand reached out towards me from the ice cliffs that were fading into the horizon. A voice begged me to stay. I saw a figure alone on the ice. He was crying. Tears spilt down his face and froze to his cheeks as he cried out to the ship. He sank to his knees, bowed his head and clasped his snow-filled hands to his face in despair. The crystal powder spilt through his beard and down his body. He raised his head and took one long last look at the ship before he became one with the ice, and I was left with just his memory. The image of his tortured face is with me forever, every time I see my reflection.

Sitting here day after day with the same stupid, sick people,
The same bloody room and grease on the knives,
Because the gashman can't be bothered to clean up properly.

The BC's a fucking moron,
He thinks he's a general in the fucking army

If that cunt Alan keeps staring at me at dinner,
With his wide-open mouth full of shit,
I'm going to puke.

And if Graham starts on again
About fucking racing in the Isle of Man ...

When is it going to stop blowing a fucking gale for God's sake!
I need air ... I need to get out!
Get me off this fucking base
And away from these cunts before I go mad!

But then the storm abated and the sun shone over Antarctica,
And everything felt good.

We raced for our skis and the cold air filled our lungs,
Our hearts and our very souls.

We screamed with joy and raced about in the snow like March hares
... Until the next storm kept everyone inside again

THE END

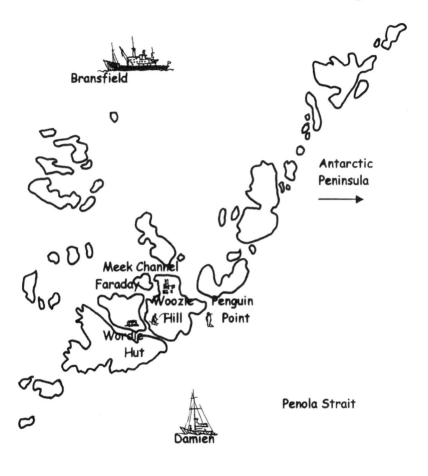

French Passage

Bransfield

Antarctic
Peninsula

Meek Channel
Faraday
Woozle
Hill
Penguin
Point
Wordie
Hut

Penola Strait

Damien

3 km.

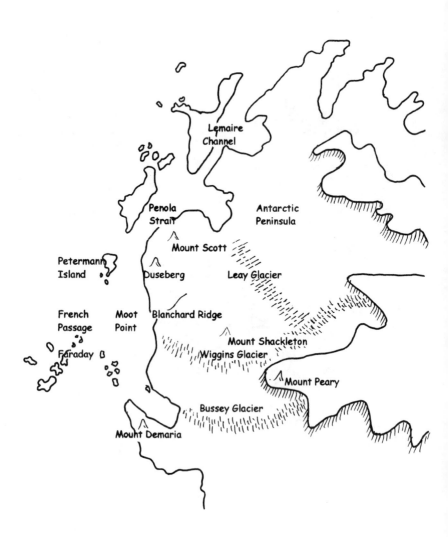